THE
BOOK
OF
HARRY

CHARLOTTE
McLAREN

THE BOOK OF HARRY

A CELEBRATION

HarperCollins*Publishers*

HarperCollins*Publishers*
1 London Bridge Street
London SE1 9GF

www.harpercollins.co.uk

HarperCollins*Publishers*
1st Floor, Watermarque Building,
Ringsend Road
Dublin 4, Ireland

First published by
HarperCollins*Publishers* 2021

10 9 8 7 6 5 4 3 2

Illustrations by Amelia Field

A catalogue record of this book
is available from the British
Library

ISBN 978-0-00-848701-0

Printed and bound by PNB, Latvia

MIX
Paper from
responsible sources
FSC™ C007454

FSC
www.fsc.org

This book is produced from
independently certified FSC™
paper to ensure responsible forest
management.

For more information visit:
www.harpercollins.co.uk/green

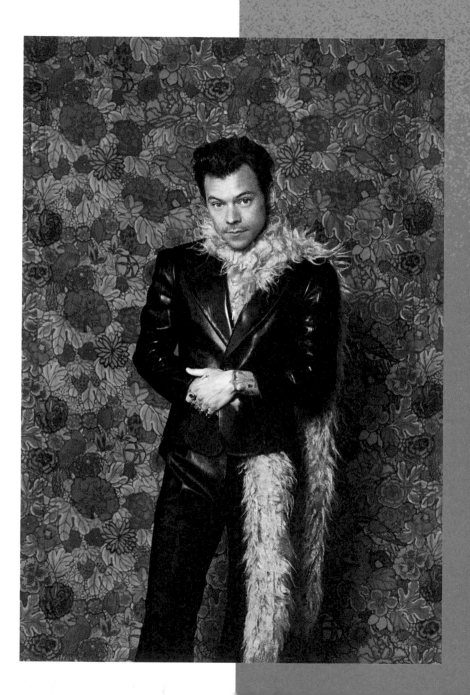

Contents

ADORE YOU

A love letter to Harry

All fans of Harry Styles know that there are many reasons why he's loved and appreciated around the world. He isn't well liked just because he has a pretty face, has good hair, happens to sing well, can act and – deep breath – was a member of one of the most famous boy bands of all time. There's so much more to him than that, as any self-respecting fan will tell you. And Harry has a variety of fans, young and old. Some fans appreciate the way Harry looks – as if he has just time-travelled from the Seventies – and younger fans love his solo material because it's such a breath of fresh air in a chart that often feels like it is overwhelmed by viral TikTok songs.

One Direction made brilliant pop music, which became slightly rockier as time went on. But when the hiatus happened, Harry emerged as a rock star with an acclaimed debut album. *Rolling Stone* magazine heralded him as a 'true rock-and-roll prince, a sunshine superman, a cosmic dancer in touch with his introspective, acoustic side'. And, if anything, his second solo album received even more positive reviews. People who hadn't previously taken One Direction seriously – no, we don't know why either! – could even admit that they loved Harry's solo music, which is a real testament to how good it is. He even won a Grammy for Best Pop Performance for 'Watermelon Sugar' in 2021 (which he performed while wearing an incredible leather suit, complete with a green feather boa).

It's undeniable that Harry is an incredibly talented singer, but he's also an amazing songwriter; he co-wrote loads of One Direction's catchiest hits, and along with the songs on his two solo albums, he's also written for other artists. He's even behind the Ariana Grande song 'Just a Little Bit of Your Heart'. And Ariana has also praised his talent: 'People know Harry, of course, first and foremost as a singer, but I think they'll be very impressed when they hear his writing skills.'

Another reason Harry stands out in the world of celebrity is because he doesn't feel like he has to follow trends. He is so loved because he is so authentically himself, and he always has been – from the days when he was a bright-eyed member of One Direction, thrust into the spotlight during *The X Factor,* wearing onesies in paparazzi shots, to now, when he's selling out arenas.

But, of course, one of the main indicators that Harry stays true to himself is his fun approach to fashion. While most of us worry about what people might think or say if we wear something a bit over the top, Harry doesn't care. He just thinks, suit yourself, and wears it anyway, meaning he shines with confidence, whatever he wears. His wardrobe is so rich and varied because he doesn't feel restricted by boring gender norms. To Harry, it doesn't matter if he found something in the women's section of a store – if he likes it, he'll wear it. In the case of the Grammys, he rocked not one, not two, but three different feather boas. And looked incredible in each of them.

But this approach to gender norms doesn't just apply to clothes – he embraces femininity wholeheartedly. 'I didn't grow up in a man's-man world,' he said, speaking to the actor Timothée Chalamet for *i-D* magazine. 'I grew up with my mum and my sister. But I definitely think, in the last two years, I've become a lot more content with who I am. I think there's so much masculinity in being vulnerable and allowing yourself to be feminine, and I'm very comfortable with that.'

Harry's always had a quiet, cheeky confidence and self-assurance – but, importantly, this confidence comes without being big-headed or arrogant. In interviews, he comes across as somebody you'd want to be friends with, as he'd be genuinely interested in hearing about your day. In fact, in a 2019 interview in the *Guardian*, writer Tom Lamont remembers that he interviewed Harry during his One Direction days, and when Harry spotted the journalist in a café a week later, Tom says that the singer invited him over to join his friends.

Because he is grounded, humble and down to earth, Harry is kind. 'Treat People With Kindness' isn't just a song for Harry; it's the way he's always lived his life. He isn't nice in an inauthentic way, as a way to try to get himself some good publicity; he doesn't shout about many of the lovely things he does, expecting to get praise, he just does them instead. One of Harry's friends – Ed Sheeran, casual! – is reported to have told *The Mirror* that '[Harry] spent two or three grand on Domino's pizza and drove around giving them out to homeless people.' It's an incredible story, but if Ed hadn't said that in an interview, nobody would have known.

He also has time for his fans, and never belittles them or acts as if they're not important. Throughout his decade in the spotlight, Harry has continued to show his fans respect, knowing that, despite his incredible talent, he owes them his career. He stands up for them too, regularly speaking about how amazing young women are – telling *Rolling Stone* that girls are 'our future – our future doctors, lawyers, mothers, presidents … Young girls like The Beatles,' he said. 'You gonna tell me they're not serious? How can you say young girls don't get it?'

Speaking of The Beatles, during One Direction's hiatus, he has also never said anything negative about being in the band. Of course, Harry understands that without 1D, he wouldn't be where he is today – and being in the band from the age of 16 taught him everything he knows about the wild world of fame and the music industry. 'I think the typical thing is to come out of a band like that and almost feel like you have to apologise for being in it, but I loved my time in it,' he told US *Vogue*. 'It was all new to me, and I was trying to learn as much as I could.'

And from waving Pride flags onstage to attending a Black Lives Matter protest in Los Angeles, to speaking about feminism and mental health, Harry has tried to make his fans feel loved and supported. He has previously said he wants his concerts to be places where anyone feels welcome to be who they are. 'I want to make people feel comfortable being whatever they want to be,' he said in an interview with *Rolling Stone*. 'Maybe at a show you can have a moment of knowing that you're not alone.' He refuses to define his own sexuality when interviewers ask, showing that you don't have to use labels if you don't want to.

He's also very, very funny, as his stint as a host on *Saturday Night Live* proved. Even Fleetwood Mac's Stevie Nicks – one of Harry's best mates, no big deal – thinks he deserves his own TV show 'like James Corden or Johnny Carson', because he's that hilarious. (You might remember that in 2017 Harry actually did take over *The Late Late Show* when James Corden's wife went into labour just hours before the host was due to go on air.)

For those who have been fans since his One Direction days, you will know that Harry's always been a joker, from playing Marcel in the 'Best Song Ever' video to his bemused expressions during TV interviews (one of the funniest being when One Direction played Never Have I Ever with Ellen DeGeneres, when most of the questions just happened to revolve mostly around Harry). Yes, there are lists of Harry's best fashion moments, but it would be just as easy to compile a list of all his funniest quips.

So, thank you for all the laughs, Harry, thank you for the music, the incredible fashion #looks. And thank you for all the other reasons why we love you (there are too many to list, if we're being honest!). But, mainly, thank you for always being yourself, and for being so kind to your fans. We'll always appreciate and support you.

'I WANT
PEOPLE
COMFO
BE
WHAT
THEY
TO

TO MAKE FEEL RTABLE ING EVER WANT BE'

16

Introduction

We think Harry Styles might be one of the coolest
men in the world, and we can all try to be a bit more
like him. We promise, it really isn't as hard as it
looks! This book will look at the way Harry lives his
life and how he has become so successful and then,
through tips and tricks, it will show you easy ways
to be more like the superstar. That might include
embracing your own personal style, maintaining
friendships or helping charities. It will also show
how you too can 'Treat People With Kindness'. So,
what are you waiting for? Get stuck in, and soon you
will be spreading kindness wherever you go.

HISTORY

Harry's journey from the bakery to superstardom

The start of it all

We might know Harry today as a rock-and-roll star and
Gucci poster boy, more likely to be compared to Mick Jagger
than McFly. (Not that there's anything wrong with McFly,
of course!) But Harry wasn't always selling out arenas. It's
very easy to forget that the singer started his career on the
UK singing competition *The X Factor*, just like Little Mix,
Leona Lewis and Olly Murs, as part of the newly formed
boy band One Direction. In 2010, over a decade ago, nobody
could have quite predicted the band's longevity and success
– even though girls used to camp outside the *X Factor* house
in London, desperate to catch a glimpse of Harry and his
bandmates.

You won't be surprised to find out that, pre-*X Factor*,
Harry always had an interest in singing. As a child, he
recorded covers on a karaoke machine he was given by his
grandfather – the first song he recorded was Elvis Presley's
'The Girl of My Best Friend' – and when he was at school in
Holmes Chapel, a village in Cheshire, he was the lead singer
of a group called White Eskimo. Perhaps a sign of what was
to come, the group even won the school's Battle of the Bands
competition.

This, along with encouragement from his mother, Anne,
meant that Harry decided to audition for *The X Factor*. The
audition video, which has now been viewed millions of
times on YouTube, sees Harry already looking stylish in a
grey cardigan, expertly styled with a skinny scarf. 'I work
in a bakery,' a young Harry says, when judge Simon Cowell
asks him to tell the audience a bit about himself. (The owner

of the W. Mandeville bakery later said they had never had an employee as polite as Harry!) Harry also told the crowd that he had just finished his GCSEs, and he would be going back to college to study law, sociology, business 'and something else, but I'm not sure yet'. Obviously, this didn't go entirely to plan ... Harry blew everyone – apart from judge Louis Walsh – away with his a cappella performance of Stevie Wonder's 'Isn't She Lovely'.

Louis was apprehensive – he worried that Harry was too young and needed more experience, which Simon Cowell told him was a load of 'rubbish', and that the whole point

'I WORK IN A BAKERY'

of the competition was to find a star, whether or not they needed a bit of training. Simon and Nicole Scherzinger saw the beginnings of a superstar and gave enthusiastic yeses. And when Louis said no, Simon joked that the audience didn't boo loud enough.

One Direction

So then Harry was through to boot camp, the next stage of the competition. But boot camp wasn't so easy and, despite his best efforts, he didn't make it any further in the Boys category. (The Boys category was for young men aged 16–25.) We probably don't need to tell you what happened next … Nicole had the genius idea of putting Harry in a group with other solo auditionees Niall Horan, Zayn Malik, Liam Payne and Louis Tomlinson. 'This is a life line,' Simon said, when he delivered the news, 'you have a real shot here.' And so, One Direction – one of the most famous groups of all time – was born, with Harry even coming up with the ingenious name.

At judges' houses, there was an unexpected hurdle for the boys to jump when Louis was taken to hospital after being stung by a sea urchin. Ouch! The accident could have derailed their whole performance, as it impacted their rehearsal time, but thankfully it didn't. The newly formed group delivered an impressive version of Natalie Imbruglia's karaoke classic 'Torn' to Simon and his guest judge, Sinitta. One Direction weren't entirely polished, but they already looked, and sounded, like the beginnings of a perfect boy band.

Following their debut on the show, it didn't take long for the UK to fall in love with the band. The entire group's popularity was proven week after week, as they made it to the final. Their first performance on the live shows was singing 'Viva La Vida' by Coldplay, but they went on to nail hits like Rihanna's 'Only Girl (In the World)' and Bonnie Tyler's 'Total Eclipse of the Heart', and in the final they performed 'She's the One' with Robbie Williams. Harry's village continued to cheer him on, and signs were held up in the bakery where he worked. But fans obviously didn't just adore the group's performances. Their video diaries from

the show have now been watched millions of times, as the boys messed and joked around (the clips were nearly always filmed on a stairway). In their second one, Louis said Liam was the smart one, Harry was the flirt (he said this with a wink), 'Zayn is vain,' Niall is the funny one – Harry then said Louis was the leader, because there was 'nothing left'. The videos, with moments such as Zayn saying 'vas happenin' and Louis joking that he liked girls who liked carrots, have become the stuff of *X Factor* legend.

We all know One Direction didn't win the competition, but of course it didn't matter. *The X Factor* was only the beginning – something that most groups on the show can't boast. After the series, they published their first book, *One Direction: Forever Young (Our Official X Factor Story),* and then they released their first single, 'What Makes You Beautiful', in September 2011. A couple of months later, *Up All Night,* their first album, became the fastest-selling debut album of 2011 in the UK – and they were also signed by Columbia Records in North America.

Fame and fortune awaits

The stage was set for superstardom, and the boys more than delivered. One Direction became one of the bestselling boy bands of all time – as of 2020, they've sold a whopping 70 million records – with fans across the planet. They toured the world, packing out stadiums. They even released their own movie, *This Is Us,* directed by acclaimed filmmaker Morgan Spurlock, which followed their 2012/13 tour.

'THE INTERNET'S FIRST BOY BAND'

As a five-piece band, they released four albums packaged with chart-topping singles, and have won over 200 awards – including 28 Teen Choice Awards. The hysteria that followed them was regularly compared to that for The Beatles, and the band broke one of the iconic group's records when they had five Top 10 debut tracks on the Hot 100 compared to The Beatles' four.

Despite the huge number of records sold, it would be impossible to say how many bedroom walls their posters were plastered upon, how many girls cried (with happiness, of course!) at their concerts or how many people bought One Direction merch – everything from T-shirts to dolls.

They were one of the biggest things to come out of the 2010s, and they have since been labelled the internet's first boy band, thanks to their overwhelming support and love online.

Sure, being in a successful band looks like the most fun for a group of young men – but the lads worked incredibly hard for their stardom and spent the majority of their time away from their friends and family. As Harry's father Des says in the film, 'Harry went to *The X Factor* as a kid and never came home.' There's also a famous scene where Liam's mum, Karen, buys a cardboard cut-out as she says that's the only way she'll see Liam. 'He left home my little boy and became the boy in a magazine,' she said. 'If I have this, I can still see him every day.'

Zayn and the hiatus

But on 25 March 2015, things took a turn for the worse when one of the biggest entertainment stories of the twenty-first century broke: Zayn Malik was leaving One Direction. Hearts around the world were smashed into tiny pieces as the news was broadcast on TV and splashed across the front pages of newspapers. Truly, it was everywhere. While it was a huge, upsetting story, it wasn't the biggest shock; Zayn had reportedly been struggling with anxiety (which he spoke about openly after leaving the band), and he left the group's tour in Southeast Asia days before the big announcement.

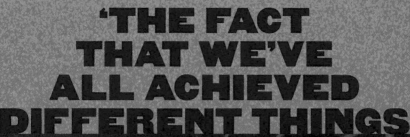

'THE FACT THAT WE'VE ALL ACHIEVED DIFFERENT THINGS

OUTSIDE OF THE BAND SAYS A LOT ABOUT HOW HARD WE WORKED IN IT'

'I am leaving because I want to be a normal 22-year-old who is able to relax and have some private time out of the spotlight,' Zayn said in a statement on social media. 'I know I have four friends for life in Louis, Liam, Harry and Niall. I know they will continue to be the best band in the world.'

Zayn was right: as a four-piece, Liam, Louis, Niall and Harry continued to be an excellent group. But Zayn's departure obviously changed the dynamic and shook the group. That night, onstage in Jakarta, Indonesia, Harry wiped away tears.

One day in the studio Harry suggested that the band might want to take a break. 'I didn't want to exhaust our fan base,' he told *Rolling Stone*. 'If you're short-sighted, you can think, "Let's just keep touring," but we all thought too much of the group to let that happen. You realise you're exhausted and you don't want to drain people's belief in you.'

A few months after Zayn's departure, in August 2015, the group announced their hiatus. Their last concert together was on 31 October at Sheffield Arena, and their last televised performance was on New Year's Eve 2015. Obviously, now, over ten years since the gang were put together, we're all still wishing for the group to reunite. And they probably will, at some point. The boys are still mates, and they looked back on their time in the group fondly on their tenth anniversary (23 July 2020). In his tribute, Harry thanked the fans – and his bandmates. 'To the boys, I love you so much, and I couldn't be prouder of everything we achieved together,' he wrote. 'Here's to ten.'

Solo star

Following the hiatus, it was time for the rest of the boys to emerge as solo stars. They've all done exceptionally well, too. Niall has released two well-received albums, Liam has released six UK Top 40 singles, Zayn now has the creative freedom he wants, and, along with a stint as a judge on *The X Factor*, Louis has also released a great album.

But despite their individual successes, Harry himself wasn't sure he would be able to achieve more dizzying career heights. Speaking on *The Ellen DeGeneres Show* in 2019, he said he originally wasn't sure whether people would still want to go and see him perform without One Direction. Obviously, he couldn't have been more wrong – but it shows that Harry isn't big-headed or arrogant. He doesn't just assume good things will come to him – he knows it takes work, a bit of risk and a sprinkle of kindness to be successful.

'Sign of the Times' was Harry's first single, which went straight to Number One in the UK chart – it was loved so much that music magazine *Rolling Stone* crowned it the best single released in 2017. The music video, filmed on the Isle of Skye, even sees Harry flying like an extra-fashionable superhero (the video was filmed without CGI, Harry was actually suspended from a helicopter!).

But his move away from the group didn't mean he was suddenly going to try to erase his history in the boy band. He loved his time in One Direction, and he doesn't mind who knows that. And that's what Harry told Beatles' legend Paul McCartney, who interviewed Styles for his first cover shoot

YOU ARE AT YOUR MOST CREATIVE WHEN YOU STOP WORRYING ABOUT MAKING MISTAKES

with *Another Man* following the hiatus. 'The nice thing for me is that I'm not coming away from the band feeling like I wasn't able to do what I wanted to do,' he said. He has never spoken ill of being in the band or dissed their music. (In the past, he's said he works out listening to One Direction's old hits!) And he's always tried to dispel any rumours of rivalry.

He's also said that he doesn't feel the need to compare his success with any of his bandmates' solo careers, respecting that Niall, Liam, Louis and Zayn have their own individual achievements and differing styles as solo artists. And that's OK. In fact, when Zayn made comments about not liking One Direction's music, Harry didn't attack him; instead, he wished him all the best, telling *Rolling Stone* in 2017 that 'it's a shame he felt that way', but that he wished Zayn nothing but luck, because he was now doing what he loved. 'I think there's a want to pit people against each other. And I think it's never been about that for us,' he told *Variety* in 2020. 'It's about a next step in evolution. The fact that we've all achieved different things outside of the band says a lot about how hard we worked in it.' He has also said that the band taught him a lot, and that their constant touring is probably the reason he enjoys travelling so much now – in fact, he told *Vogue* he was considering a temporary move to Tokyo in the future.

Pivotally, Harry has always allowed himself space to grow. Looking back, he has said he was 'very much finding out what my sound was as a solo artist' when he was recording his self-titled debut album, saying he 'let go of the fear of getting it wrong' on his second album. He told *Vogue* that the process was 'really joyous and really free'. As the superstar says, you are at your most creative when you stop worrying about making mistakes. Like Harry, you always have the opportunity to evolve and reinvent yourself.

TREAT PEOPLE WITH KINDNESS

A mantra for life

When Harry met Phoebe

After a year of uncertainty, on New Year's Day 2021, Harry treated his fans – and the world – to 3 minutes and 21 seconds of pure joy when he dropped the video to 'Treat People With Kindness'. But he didn't do it alone. Harry recruited a very special guest for the video: the *Fleabag* actress and writer Phoebe Waller-Bridge.

During the black-and-white video, the pair joyously danced around the Troxy theatre in East London, wearing matching sweater vests and Gucci suits, with Harry styled in a bedazzled blazer. The video perfectly captured the song: happy, soulful and upbeat. Harry and Phoebe were an unlikely collaboration, but that made the whole thing even more fun. (For those wondering why Harry and Phoebe worked together, Harry went to see Phoebe perform during London's theatre run of *Fleabag* – and, bam, the rest is history.)

The collaboration, and the dancing – which was inspired by Old Hollywood dancers like the Nicholas Brothers and Fred Astaire – might have been a surprise. But 'Treat People With Kindness' is nothing new to Harry's legion of loyal fans. During the promotion of his second album, before anything was officially announced, eagled-eyed fans knew something was on the way when they spotted billboards with the TPWK acronym. Those four letters are the ethos by which Harry lives his life, and luckily it's something we can all strive to incorporate into our everyday lives.

The start of TPWK

Though Harry has always been kind, he didn't intend for
TPWK to become the wonderful movement that it has.
Harry wore 'TPWK' as a pin on his guitar strap when he was
touring, and he then created T-shirts for the mantra as tour
merchandise, including Pride T-shirts sold to raise funds
for charity. It all snowballed from there.

He then wrote the anthem 'Treat People With Kindness'
with songwriters Jeff Bhasker and Ilsey Juber, which was
one of the last songs put together for the album *Fine Line*.
Surprisingly, Harry wasn't entirely sure about the track at
first. He's previously revealed that he didn't know whether
he loved or hated it, but he felt inspired after watching
another interview with a very famous icon. 'I'd seen this
clip of David Bowie talking, saying that you usually end
up doing your best work when you feel like you can't quite
touch the bottom, and realising that the fact it made me
feel a little uncomfortable didn't mean it was a bad song,'
he said. Proof that, like David and Harry, sometimes you
have to move slightly outside your comfort zone to achieve
great things!

According to Harry, the song is all about small changes
making a big difference and 'being a lot nicer to each other',
rather than telling people not to do things. And hopefully,
during this chapter, we'll arm you with all the little ways
you can help make a monumental difference to others –
while improving your own life at the same time.

If, unlike Harry, you're still not completely convinced
that kindness makes the world go round, it's worth

knowing that there are proven health benefits to being kind. As well as brightening up everyone around you, it can help you feel better too. Kindness increases oxytocin production, which is said to be responsible for feelings of happiness. It's also thought that kindness can boost levels of serotonin, which is responsible for mood regulation and general wellbeing. Pretty cool, right? It also has benefits for memory, learning and brain function. According to research from Emory University, in Atlanta, when you are kind to another person, your brain's pleasure and reward centres light up – as if you were the person on the other side of the good deed. And hey, some even claim that being kind can help you live longer.

SMALL CHANGES MAKE A BIG DIFFERENCE

TREAT OTHERS AS YOU WISH TO BE TREATED

Even though he's one of the most famous men alive, Harry has never let fame go to his head. There are countless stories of Harry asking to get tea for people working backstage and buying food for his fans who have been patiently waiting for him before concerts. In a 2019 interview in the *Guardian*, he said he thinks 'what's yer excuse?' when he meets successful people who aren't nice.

Director Gabe Turner, who has worked with Harry since the days of One Direction and directed the 'TPWK' video attests to his kind nature. He said, in an interview with *Grazia* magazine, that Harry has always made an effort to make every person on set 'feel ten foot tall'. Even though he could probably get away with it if he wanted to, Harry isn't a famous diva on set, throwing tantrums and making unreasonable demands. It's a cliché, but teamwork really does make the dream work – if ever you're working as a group, treat everyone as you'd wish to be treated. And encourage others. Thank other people when they've done a good job too.

Probably one of the reasons why Harry and Phoebe Waller-Bridge got along so well during the 'TPWK' shoot was their work ethic, and their belief that you should treat everybody as equals – reportedly, the actress even bought cupcakes for everyone. Harry and Phoebe are proof that you can be incredibly powerful, while still being incredibly sweet. Kindness isn't a weakness – and don't let anybody try to tell you otherwise.

RANDOM ACTS OF KINDNESS

But, of course, Harry isn't just nice when he's working. A superfan was in for a shock last year when Harry's car broke down outside her house. Sadly, Theadora, the fan, wasn't in – but, while Harry waited for his car to be sorted, her dad invited him in for a cup of tea. When Harry found out that his host's daughter was a fan, he wrote Theadora a note, saying he was 'devastated' to have missed her. He signed the note: 'P.S. I fed the fish.' A photo of the sweet note and Harry feeding the fish quickly went viral. Theadora apparently cried when she realised that she'd missed the superstar's visit – but luckily on the note Harry wrote: 'Tell your dad to get in touch, and I'll see you at a show.'

Like Harry, we can all aim to do more sweet things for people. You don't have to buy your colleagues cupcakes like Phoebe, or feed someone's fish like Harry – but maybe you can incorporate more random acts of kindness into your life.

Feeling inspired? We're sure you can come up with your own ways to brighten someone else's day, but if you need a little help:

- Plant a tree to help the environment – or pick up rubbish around town.
- Clean your room or a shared area. (Bonus points if you haven't been asked!)
- Send a nice message to a friend, for absolutely no reason. You could even tell them their best qualities – who doesn't want to hear that? They might really need it.
- Even better, you could call them – and always make sure to listen to their problems.
- If you think someone is feeling a bit left out, befriend them. Everybody knows what it's like to be a bit shy, or to feel like you don't fit in – maybe you can help somebody else?
- Has somebody done something to help you? Make sure to send them a thank-you note. Manners are important – and underrated.

RESPECT

Of course, it goes without saying that you make far more friends through being kind and focusing on the good in other people. Sometimes the kindest thing to do, even if someone has upset you in the past, is to forgive them and let a grudge go.

And if you are kind, this also means you have to respect other people. For example, Harry always treats his fans with kindness and never belittles them. He never mocks young women for loving pop music, supporting his career and singing and dancing at gigs. He recognises how wonderful it is to be a fan and to be part of a community. When Harry was asked about his changing solo sound, and audience, in a *Rolling Stone* interview, the musician defended his younger fans. 'They kind of keep the world going,' Harry told the interviewer. 'Teenage-girl fans – they don't lie. If they like you, they're there. They don't act "too cool". They like you, and they tell you. Which is sick.'

'I'LL WAIT FOR YOU'

As well as defending their taste, Harry is also there to support his community of fans, which is something we can all learn from. During a show in London, he saw a fan having a panic attack and immediately asked the crowd to help her. In 2019, when a fan he follows on Twitter tweeted: 'I guess therapy can wait ... HS2 and tour can't,' he replied, 'Go to therapy, it's important. I'll wait for you. #WorldMentalHealth.' Harry himself goes to therapy, he says, 'not every week, but whenever I feel I need it'.

This is the kind of open attitude we should all have surrounding mental health – if you know one of your friends is struggling, make sure to let them know you are there for them. Sometimes it can be as easy as asking somebody how they are (always ask twice, though, as people are more likely to tell you how they're really feeling if you ask again). Also, if you are having trouble with your own mental health, make sure to confide in someone you trust. If this is not available to you, there are charities, such as

AUTHEN-TICITY AND KINDNESS NEVER GO OUT OF FASHION

the Samaritans, who run helplines you can contact. Don't suffer in silence; you are not alone. As Harry says, it's always important to reach out if you need to.

But sometimes, when you're empathetic and want to help others, it can be all too easy to forget about yourself. However, to be the best version of yourself, you have to take the time to look after yourself – whether that's doing new things or taking some time out to rest. As the old saying goes, you can't pour from an empty cup. And Harry practises self-care, too. He said in an interview with Radio 1Xtra that he had been taking the time to do face masks and learn new skills, such as Italian and sign language, during the coronavirus pandemic.

IF YOU NEED SOME
IDEAS FOR SELF-CARE:

- Have a nice relaxing bath, complete with bubble bath or a bath bomb.
- Take some time away from social media if you feel like you need some space. You could also edit your account, to make sure you're only following accounts that make you feel positive.
- Get dressed up and wear a fancy outfit for no reason other than because you want to!
- Binge-watch your favourite TV show and don't feel guilty about it.
- Blast some Harry and have a dance on your own. Don't feel silly; not only is dancing good exercise, it is also proven to make you feel better and reduce stress.
- Try something creative and learn a new skill … (This could be an excuse to learn knitting and get on your way to creating Harry's JW Anderson cardigan. But more on that later …)
- To put you in a more positive mood, you could even write down a list of things you are grateful for each day. You don't have to buy a fancy gratitude journal – just use a notebook and get writing. There are even apps you can download on your phone.
- There are also apps like Calm, which can help you meditate and get to sleep. Harry even recorded a story for the app to help you drift off.

CHOOSE KINDNESS EVERY DAY

Being kind isn't just about random acts of kindness. As Harry knows, it's something you choose to be every day – whether you realise it or not. Here are some ideas to incorporate kindness into your daily life.

1. Do something nice for someone else in the morning. Whether that's making someone a cup of tea/coffee or breakfast, or sending a morning message to someone. Not only does this start your day on a positive note, but it'll make somebody else's day brighter too.

2. Smile! Not just to friends and random people you encounter; smile for yourself … Experts say that smiling releases endorphins, natural painkillers and serotonin, making you feel happier.

3. Look to see where you can help others in everyday encounters. Can you see somebody struggling with their shopping? Does somebody on the bus need your seat more than you? Do you have any spare change to give to charity or a homeless person?

4. Reach out to your friends to check in and make sure they're alright. Reminding your friends and family that you love and appreciate them never goes amiss.

5. Give everyone a chance – and don't judge a book by its cover. Let go of the assumptions you have about people.

6. Take some time for yourself every day to do something for you. (If you need inspiration, look at our self-care list opposite!) You could also use this time to reflect on when you've been kind to others and to think about how you can do the same tomorrow.

As we hope you've discovered, there really are so many benefits to being kind – it makes other people feel better, and, if we're being a bit selfish, it makes us happier too. We're sure you're already lovely, but kindness is something you can always get better at – even if that means just sprinkling a few more random acts of kindness into your life and showing yourself some more love. Authenticity and kindness never go out of fashion, as we're sure Harry would tell you.

'Any time you can make someone who potentially might not feel as great about themselves as they should feel better about themselves, I think that's always a positive thing.'

SIGN OF THE TIMES

Harry's style school

50

With 'style' quite literally in his name, it seems Harry Styles was destined to become the fashion star he is today. With a personal style that somehow manages to be feminine, flamboyant and fierce all at the same time, from the age of 19, when he won a trophy at the British Fashion Awards, Harry has been regarded as one of the most fashionable men in the world.

If somebody doesn't know Harry for his music – and, come on, we all know they should – then it's likely they'll be able to list at least one of his most iconic fashion moments. The pink shirt and high-waisted white trousers he wore on the cover of his second album, *Fine Line*; the string of pearls around his neck at the BRIT Awards in 2020; the Princess Diana-inspired sheep jumper-vest he wore in New York; the dress he rocked on the cover of *Vogue* (more on that later). And that's just to name a few!

In fact, Harry loves clothes so much that it's reported he keeps his outfits in pristine condition by storing them in a vault, where they are cryogenically frozen. His fresh take on fashion, and his ability to blend jewellery, tuxedo suits and heeled boots, means that, following his break from One Direction, Harry was taken seriously by the fashion world. Of course, we loved his style in the group, but even that evolved. His dress sense in One Direction grew up from the *X Factor* days of onesies and Jack Wills hoodies to a clean-cut boy-band member in preppy blazers, before moving on to his rockier phase, complete with longer hair, styled with bandanas.

The boy with the pearl earring

But, in 2019, things really changed for Harry when he was invited to become the face of Gucci's tailoring campaign. The photos of him in an extravagant suit, cradling hens in a fish-and-chip shop in the quiet town of St Albans, sent the internet into overdrive. Nobody was surprised when he was asked back for more Gucci campaigns.

But his biggest fashion achievement to date is, no doubt, when he was invited to co-chair the 2019 Met Gala by Anna Wintour, the editor of American *Vogue*, along with Lady Gaga, tennis player Serena Williams and Gucci's creative director Alessandro Michele. The annual event is the biggest on the fashion calendar, when the most illustrious stars in fashion, music and film gather to mark the start of the Costume Institute's annual fashion exhibit. The exhibition and gala's theme was Camp: Notes on Fashion – based around Susan Sontag's 1964 essay 'Notes on "Camp"', which considers what the word 'camp' means – and Harry's fans held their breath as they wondered what he would wear to the prestigious party.

Obviously, Harry did not disappoint. He stunned in a black, ruffled lace shirt, with high-waisted black trousers, complete with painted nails and an assortment of rings, including two with his initials H and S on them. The finishing touch was a singular pearl earring, which Harry specifically pierced his ear for – think Boy with a Pearl Earring. Editor Eva Chen, who is now head of fashion

partnerships at Instagram, said the most memorable moment of the evening was when Harry told her that he pierced his ear himself.

The look was put together by his long-term stylist, Harry Lambert, and Gucci's Alessandro. In an interview with *Vogue*, Lambert explained the slightly subdued, yet nonetheless surprising look. 'I think everyone was expecting Harry to be in sequins, bright colours and a crown, but we decided on a different type of "camp" that hopefully would surprise,' he said, explaining why Harry turned his back on the florals he was wearing on tour. 'This look is about taking traditionally feminine elements like the frills, heeled boots, sheer fabric and the pearl earring, but then rephrasing them as masculine pieces set against the high-waisted tailored trousers and his tattoos. The look, I feel, is elegant. It's camp, but still Harry.'

Harry – 1, Gender norms – 0

And this is what Harry and his team do so well. Blending the masculine and the feminine into looks that challenge outdated – and boring – gender norms. It was ground-breaking enough when Harry appeared as the first solo male on the cover of US *Vogue* in 2020, but he decided to shake things up further by wearing a beautiful frothy blue dress designed by Gucci.

It shouldn't have been controversial. Drag queens have been fashionably pushing the boundaries for years. And

'BRING BACK MANLY MEN'

popstars like Prince, David Bowie and Freddie Mercury have been wearing feminine clothes and make-up for decades. But, for some reason, a minority of people were shocked that a man was wearing a dress. US conservative writer Candace Owens saw the pictures as an 'attack' on Western civilisation and pleaded for society to 'bring back manly men'. In response to the furore, Harry posted a photo on Instagram, wearing a flamboyant baby-blue suit, cheekily eating a banana. The caption? 'Bring back manly men.' Harry – 1, Gender norms – 0.

Despite the controversy from a few, as Harry also says in his *Vogue* cover interview, luckily now the 'lines are becoming more and more blurred' when it comes to men's and women's fashion. If you're a girl and you want to wear a suit, or something other people might think is a little tomboy-ish: go for it. And if you're a boy and you want to wear a dress, or a skirt, or something wondrous in bubblegum pink: go for it. If anyone has a problem with that, the issue lies with them and most certainly not you. 'To not wear [something] because it's females' clothing, you shut out a whole world of great clothes,' Harry says.

How to have fun with your clothes

You don't have to have a huge interest in fashion – or a stylist to the stars on speed dial – to embody a bit of Harry Styles in your wardrobe. The secret is: you just have to embrace who you are and wear what you want. (So long as it's not actually offensive – treat people with kindness, remember?)

But, most importantly, you have to have fun. You don't have to get it right every time, and that's the beauty of it. Fashion is all about experimenting and finding what's right for you. Harry says his playful approach to fashion is thanks to Lambert, as he has 'fun with clothing' and 'doesn't take it too seriously'.

According to Harry, there's no such thing as overdressing either. 'Now I'll put on something that feels really flamboyant, and I don't feel crazy wearing it,' he told *Vogue.* 'I think if you get something that you feel amazing in, it's like a superhero outfit.' It's an admirable attitude. If you want to be more Harry, basically don't be afraid of looking extra. Remember, wearing bold outfits requires a level of confidence that most people would love to have (even if they can't always admit it, because they're jealous!).

Work with what you already have

If you are thinking about giving your wardrobe a shake-up, like Harry did when he started his solo career, it might be the perfect time to consider your personal style. Don't worry – you don't need to have a designer budget or to buy tons of new clothes to embrace your true self. But you do have to be thoughtful and inventive.

Start with what you already have. Think about what you enjoy wearing most ... What are your favourite items in your wardrobe? Maybe it's a bright dress, a pair of jeans or even a Harry Styles T-shirt – what makes you feel the happiest when you wear it, like you are the best version of yourself? What are your favourite colours? What makes you smile? Gravitate towards these clothes, and you might even be rewarded by becoming more confident. Psychologists even say that if we feel good in what we're wearing, we're likely to be more confident. How amazing is that? – fashion isn't just frivolous, it's powerful. You could jot down your favourite things here.

_____

_____

_____

_____

_____

_____

Most importantly, when you're working out your
personal style, don't feel too swayed by trends – being
happy in something is far more important than wearing
something just because you think it will get likes on
Instagram. Trends change all the time – and items nearly
always come back into fashion (hello, flares) – so it can be
overwhelming, and sometimes pointless, to keep up. Plus,
it's far more fun to start your own trends, à la Harry.

How to make
a mood board

Even trendsetters sometimes need inspiration. You don't
have to be a fashion designer or to have studied textiles at
school to use a mood board to inspire you. A mood board is a
collage that will help guide your style – and you don't have
to be limited to photos of clothes you like or celebrities
wearing fun outfits. The best part is you can include
pictures of anything that inspires you. A pretty sunset,

your favourite city, a black-and-white photo from another era, even your favourite sweets. The possibilities are endless. All you need is a pinboard and some glue or Blu Tack to stick down some images. Here's how to do it …

- Make sure you have a few hours free – and have Harry or One Direction's music playing, obviously!
- If you have some magazines, these are a great place to cut out images from – have a look through and see if there's anything that inspires you. (Also, recycling is kind to the planet.)
- But don't limit yourself to what's in the pages. Feel free to print off pictures of places, people and outfits you'd like to include.
- Maybe write down a few of Harry's best fashion quotes, too – if anybody can inspire you, it's him!
- Place everything in front of you before you start sticking everything down, so you have a clear idea of what your mood board will look like.
- Get sticking! And make sure your board is hanging somewhere you can see it, so it can always help you if you're lacking inspiration.

Or, if this sounds a bit too messy, don't worry: you can do it by saving images online and creating a digital mood board

How to spring clean your wardrobe

So, hopefully by you now you have worked out what you already love. But, if you want, it might make sense to use the opportunity to get rid of a few things from your wardrobe. Don't worry if you don't have any clothes you don't want to get rid of – this step is totally optional.

1. Take all of your clothes out of your wardrobe. When we can't see everything, we often forget some of the things that are lying at the back of drawers. This might take a lot of effort – get some Harry on to motivate you.
2. When you're considering whether to get rid of an item, ask yourself a few questions. Is it practical? Do I like it? Do I wear it a lot? Does it mean something to me? Answer yes to any of these and the item should go into a 'keep' pile. Those clothes that maybe aren't in the best condition can go into a 'get rid of' pile. And clothes that are in good enough condition to give away can go into a 'donate' pile.
3. Check where you can donate your clothes. For the ones that aren't in good enough condition to give away, find out if you can recycle the fabric. Some stores even let you take in a bag of clothes, which they can recycle, in return for a discount.
4. Then clean wherever you keep your clothes, and make sure everything goes back tidily.

'I THINK IF YOU GET SOMETHING THAT YOU FEEL AMAZING IN IT'S LIKE A SUPERHERO OUTFIT.'

Knit happens

Good news if you're a superfan: you can also re-create one of Harry's most famous outfits. (Warning: you might need a lot of patience.) When Harry rehearsed for the *TODAY* show in February 2020, photos of him wearing a gorgeous patchwork cardigan went viral – and the bright, Seventies-inspired cardi quickly sold out (yes, even though it cost £1,250). But worry not. The designer, JW Anderson, shared the pattern so fans could make it themselves, saying he was 'impressed and incredibly humbled' by fans recreating the quirky look. So, if you've got time on your hands, learn to knit – and then take yourself to YouTube and find the JW tutorial. (FYI, it's called JW Anderson | Official 'Harry Styles' Cardigan Knitting Tutorial.) Knitting is cool, we promise.

Don't limit yourself

So, have fun! As Harry knows, fashion isn't supposed to be something you're scared of getting wrong. Don't limit yourself. Push boundaries and enjoy yourself. Your style is supposed to evolve, and you can always reinvent yourself – you don't have to be famous or to have been in the most famous boy band of all time. The best thing is, if you have this open-minded attitude, you're already a bit like Harry. (Even if you don't quite have the money to keep your clothes in a vault.) Take a deep breath and put your most fashionable foot forward – and don't worry if your feet are in 'silly' shoes!

GOLDEN

Harry's lessons in equality and inclusion

'It's impossible not to be aware of what's going on in the world'

Living his life by the mantra 'Treat People With Kindness', it comes as no surprise that Harry tries his best to make all of his fans feel loved and welcomed. Harry champions inclusivity and diversity, helping social causes while he can along the way. 'We're living in a time where it's impossible not to be aware of what's going on in the world,' Harry told *Call Me by Your Name* actor Timothée Chalamet in a conversation for *i-D*. 'Society has never been so divisive. It's important to stand up for what we think is right.' Harry's debut single also reflects this kind of thinking, as he said about the song's meaning: '"Sign of the Times" came from, "This isn't the first time we've been in a hard time, and it's not going to be the last time."'

That doesn't mean he's given up, though. Far from it. For the last US election, he endorsed Democrat Joe Biden, tweeting 'If I could vote in America, I'd vote with kindness' alongside a video from Joe's campaign. The power of celebrities revealing their political stance like this on social media cannot be underestimated – it makes a big difference. When Taylor Swift broke her silence around political issues in 2018 by posting a statement on Instagram, *BuzzFeed News* reported there were 65,000 voter registrations in the 24-hour period afterwards. Who knows just how many people Harry will have influenced?

Black Lives Matter

During the Black Lives Matter protests of 2020, following the horrendous killing of George Floyd, Harry joined the protests in Los Angeles. He also donated money to bail funds for arrested protestors and urged his followers to do the same. 'I do things every day without fear, because I am privileged, and I am privileged every day because I am white,' Harry wrote on his Twitter account. 'Being not racist is not enough, we must be anti-racist.' He also asked others to look inwards and educate themselves.

As Harry says, in order to be an anti-racist ally, it's pivotal to educate yourself, to learn about other people's experiences and, if you are in a place of privilege, especially due to your race, you must acknowledge that. There is a lot of information online to help you on your anti-racist journey, but you can start by following activists on social media, reading books and watching films and documentaries about social causes.

Have conversations with your family and friends, and call people out if they show bias or say something that you think is racist. If you feel uncomfortable having these talks, listen to these words from Harry: 'I had a realisation that my own comfort in the conversation has nothing to do with the problem,' he told *Variety*. 'Like, that's not enough of a reason to not have a conversation.' No form of racism is ever acceptable, including

microaggressions (an action that subtly - whether it's intentional or not - expresses a prejudiced attitude).

Life's a rainbow

Harry has long been a supporter of the LGBTQ+ community, waving Pride flags at concerts since his time in One Direction. But when a fan attended one of his solo shows with a sign that read 'I'm gonna come out to my parents because of you!!!!' he stopped the entire concert so he could help. He asked Grace, the fan, what her mum's name was – when she replied 'Tina' he asked the audience to shout: 'TINA, SHE'S GAY!' Obviously, Grace was delighted by Harry's encouragement. After the gig, she tweeted Harry, saying, 'Your continuous support of the LGBTQ+ has helped me come to love myself and feel safe.'

Speaking in his 2019 *Rolling Stone* cover interview, Harry said he waves his Pride flag as a symbol of solidarity. 'I want to make people feel comfortable being whatever they want to be,' he said. 'Maybe at a show you can have a moment of knowing that you're not alone.'

And his shows have always been a place for everyone. On a 2017 tour in Stockholm, Styles told the crowd, 'If you are Black, if you are white, if you are gay, if you are straight, if you are transgender – whoever you are, whoever you want to be, I support you. I love every single one of you.'

Harry himself refuses to define his sexuality in interviews and has asked why people care so much. An unreleased song, 'Medicine', from his first album, has Harry singing the line 'the boys and the girls are in / I mess around with him and I'm okay with it', while some fans have called 'Lights Up' a 'bisexual anthem' – the song itself was released on National Coming Out Day.

In an interview with the *Guardian*, he said he doesn't intentionally leave clues about his sexuality in his work – he just collaborates with people he wants to work with. ('Am I sprinkling in nuggets of sexual ambiguity to try and be more interesting?' he asked. 'No.') Of course, Harry – just like anybody – has no obligations to put any labels on their sexuality. It's your business, and only your business. But if you do want to put a label on your sexuality and be vocal about it, then you should feel supported, comfortable and safe doing so. It's all about your personal preference. Harry himself refuses to define his sexuality in interviews and has asked why people care so much.

Girl power

Harry is also a feminist, believing that men and women should be equal. He says the influence for this was growing up with his sister and his mother. Importantly, though, he doesn't want to take the shine away from women – and in a *Rolling Stone* interview he said he doesn't 'want a lot of credit for being a feminist'. This wasn't the first time he'd expressed his feminist views. (He has worn a 'Women are smarter' T-shirt in the past.) Harry has also supported the #HeForShe UN campaign for gender equality led by actor Emma Watson.

Respecting his female fans has been something Harry has done since the start of his career. In a 2012 radio

'WHOEVER YOU ARE, WHOEVER YOU WANT TO BE, I SUPPORT YOU'

interview, when One Direction were asked a question Harry thought was sexist, he replied: 'We feel like that objectifies women, and that's not really what we're about.' As we know, One Direction were the opposite – they were all about empowering fans (and, obviously, a lot of those were young women). When Harry was asked during promo for One Direction's most recent album if it was important that songs like 'What Makes You Beautiful' empowered fans, he answered in his typical fashion: 'I think that any time you can make someone who potentially might not feel as great about themselves as they should feel better about themselves, I think that's always a positive thing.'

Equality is essential

Harry's efforts to make his fans feel welcome has made a huge difference to many of his supporters. And when you're a person of Harry's fame, even small things like showing support on social media has a big impact. As journalist Elana Rubin wrote for website Insider: 'As a Jewish fan, it meant the world when Styles tweeted about Rosh Hashanah and Yom Kippur amid a massive rise of antisemitism.'

But, as Harry knows, believing in equal rights for everyone doesn't make you a better person and you shouldn't take credit for it – it is essential and the absolute bare minimum you can do. Otherwise how can you be expected to Treat People With Kindness?

Further reading

If you're looking for further reading material after this chapter, we've compiled a list of books that could help start your journey to learning more about equality:

WHY I'M NO LONGER TALKING TO WHITE PEOPLE ABOUT RACE, BY RENI EDDO-LODGE

In seven essays, this bestselling book looks at insidious structural and covert racism, white-washing, eradicated Black history and what race relations mean in Britain today. 'Every voice raised against racism chips away at its power,' the author says. 'We can't afford to stay silent. This book is an attempt to speak.'

NEVERTHELESS, WE PERSISTED: 48 VOICES OF DEFIANCE, STRENGTH AND COURAGE

Featuring influential voices such as Black Lives Matter co-founder Patrisse Cullors and actress Alia Shawkat, this book is a collection of essays from people who have dealt with prejudice because of their race, sexual identity or gender – and persisted.

EVERYDAY ACTIVISM: HOW TO CHANGE THE WORLD IN FIVE MINUTES, ONE HOUR OR A DAY, BY RACHEL ENGLAND

Looking to make a change but don't think you have the time? Well, *Everyday Activism* proves that even if you only have a few minutes to spare, you can still create waves.

QUEER, THERE AND EVERYWHERE: 23 PEOPLE WHO CHANGED THE WORLD, BY SARAH PRAGER

Want to get up to date on your LGBTQ+ history? Discover the stories behind 23 people – from politicians, like Theodore Roosevelt, to performers, to the gender-ambiguous Queen of

Sweden – who helped the fight for the LGBTQ+ community, with some stories you won't find in other history books.

I AM MALALA: THE GIRL WHO STOOD UP FOR EDUCATION AND WAS SHOT BY THE TALIBAN, BY MALALA YOUSAFZAI WITH CHRISTINA LAMB

Malala, the youngest ever winner of the Nobel Peace Prize, writes about her upbringing and continuous fight for women's education, which resulted in an assassination attempt when she was 15.

THIS BOOK IS ANTI-RACIST: 20 LESSONS ON HOW TO WAKE UP, TAKE ACTION AND DO THE WORK, BY TIFFANY JEWELL, ILLUSTRATED BY AURÉLIA DURAND

This book teaches the history of racism and ways in which you can be anti-racist. There are also activities at the end of every chapter to help expand what you've learnt.

HERE WE ARE: FEMINISM FOR THE REAL WORLD, EDITED BY KELLY JENSEN

This book covers 'everything from body positivity to romance to gender identity to intersectionality to the greatest girl friendships in fiction' in 44 essays and includes contributions from TV legend Mindy Kaling and Roxane Gay.

SWEET CREATURE

How to make a change

Not about the money

One of the things Harry really believes in is doing your bit for charity – and you can clearly see where he gets his kind-hearted spirit from. Harry's mum, Anne Twist, is an ardent supporter of many charities. In October 2020, she raised over £10,000 for Parkinson's UK by strapping herself to a plane for a wing walk (Anne also volunteers for the charity). But that's not all. She regularly promotes various charities and causes on her Instagram – over 2 million people follow her! – and has even climbed Mount Kilimanjaro. Impressive, to say the least.

Harry, being the kind person he is, also wants to do what he can to help out. Technically, the singer is a philanthropist – a person who seeks to promote the welfare of others, especially by the generous donation of money to good causes. Do you remember how, in the 'Treat People With Kindness' chapter, we mentioned that even Harry's TPWK merch was kind? Well, he raised a whopping $1.2 million for charity during his last tour, through donating some of the profits from merchandise and ticket sales. All of the money went to charities, with the money going to an array of causes: food banks, children's hospitals, Help Refugees and anti-gun violence charities.

Unfortunately, not all of us are arena-filling popstars. We wish we had a million in the bank to give to charity – but alas, we don't. However, there are other ways you can be charitable, without tons of cash.

- **DONATE YOUR TIME.** Find out about charities in your area that could do with volunteers. In a lot of cases, time is just as valuable to a charity. You know what they say, time is money!
- **TREAT YOURSELF — AND OTHERS.** When you're buying new things, look out for places which, like Harry, donate some of their profits to charity.
- **GIFT IT.** Instead of asking for presents on special occasions like birthdays or Christmas, you could maybe ask people to make donations to charity.
- **SET YOURSELF A CHALLENGE.** Perhaps do a fun run, learn a new skill or even climb a mountain like Anne – and use the opportunity to fundraise.
- **SIGN PETITIONS FOR IMPORTANT CAUSES.** Then, to get more signatures, share them on social media. Even if you get one of your friends to help, that's a job well done!
- **WHEN YOU'RE FOOD SHOPPING, BUY AN EXTRA ITEM THAT ISN'T ON YOUR LIST.** Maybe pick up a tin of beans, vegetables or a family bar of chocolate. Many supermarkets have a basket by the door where you can make donations to food banks, where the food is distributed to people who need it most.
- **USE A SEARCH ENGINE THAT DOES GOOD WHILE YOU BROWSE THE WEB.** Sites like Everyclick donate money to charity. Ecosia even helps plant trees. And giveWater does what it says on the tin and helps provide water to countries that need it. There are loads of others too!

Look after the planet

Along with raising tons of money for charity, Harry is also environmentally conscious and considered the impact his tour might have on the planet. His debut tour made significant water conservation efforts, saving the equivalent of 13,200 single-use plastic water bottles and recycling over 6,500 gallons of water. Like Harry, we can all make little changes to our lives to be more eco-friendly.

Looking after the planet is essential and one of the kindest things we can do to try to limit the damage of climate change. When it comes to being environmentally friendly, sometimes it can feel like the big corporations hold all the power, but no action is too small.

1. When you're throwing something away, check online whether it can be recycled. You might be surprised by some of the materials that are now recyclable.
2. Around 7.3 million tons of food is chucked away in the UK every year. Not only is that a huge waste, but food in landfill creates unnecessary carbon dioxide emissions. If you struggle with food waste, it could be worth planning your meals in advance so you know you will eat everything you buy. If, as a last resort, you still have to throw away food, it's far better to compost it.
3. Eat less meat. Meat production is one of the world's biggest contributors to carbon dioxide emissions, but we can all help to reduce this by cutting a bit more meat out of our diets. Heard of Meat-free Monday?

That could be an easy way to ease yourself into eating less meat. Still need inspiration? In his *Vogue* cover interview, Harry himself revealed that he is a pescatarian (typically meaning he doesn't eat meat but does eat fish).

4. We all know plastic is bad for the environment – it takes ages to decompose, and on top of that it can be harmful to wildlife. But with a little thought, it's easy to cut down on your own plastic use. For example, don't buy single-use water bottles, and bring a canvas bag with you when you're out shopping so you don't have to buy a flimsy plastic bag. Also, look at the packaging of things – can you buy an alternative that is packaged in something that isn't plastic?

5. Get creative and upcycle things you might have otherwise thrown away. Maybe you could keep your make-up brushes in an old candle holder, create a mood board out of old magazines (see page 58) or use some old fabric to make a hairband.

Cutting edge

Some of the charities helped by Harry's most recent tour support young cancer patients – a cause he has always felt strongly about. Remember Harry's long locks before he was in *Dunkirk*? When he decided to embrace a shorter hairstyle for the role, he posted a photo on Instagram of his hair in a chopped-off plait with the caption: 'Whoops. #Littleprincesstrust.' While he didn't say whether he was donating his hair to the charity, the organisation, which provides real-hair wigs for children suffering with hair loss, said Harry's act of kindness led to a lot of publicity, leading to more followers and donations. A reminder of how you can harness the power of social media for good, by posting about charities and causes you care about.

Oh, and if you ever fancy a haircut, you're feeling bold and you want your hair to be put to good use, the charity still accepts donations. You could even get people to sponsor you to cut your hair – double the goodness!

Volunteer

OK, so maybe you still need a little more convincing about actually donating your time to charity. We all know it can be scary embarking on a new challenge. But, amazingly, volunteering also comes with extra benefits – as well as helping a cause in need. Volunteering is thought to help make you feel better, and working with other people for a positive purpose can also boost your confidence and self-esteem. It can help to ease the effects of stress, anger and anxiety too. It's also a great thing to add to your CV or university application, as it shows you have initiative, care about others and are up for learning a new skill. *Who wouldn't want to hire or enrol you?!*

SO HOW DO YOU FIND OUT WHERE YOU CAN GIVE YOUR TIME?

Online, you can find websites that act as volunteering databases for your country or local area, where you can search volunteering opportunities by interest, activity or location. On some, you can even apply online. Before having a look, it might be a good idea to have a think about what you might like to do – maybe you want to help animals, have a cup of tea and a chat with someone who's a little lonely, or work with the homeless. Ask yourself: how can I make the biggest difference? What causes do I care about? And what will I enjoy the most? Another benefit of volunteering is that it can be really good fun, and a fab place to meet new people. Get applying!

Helping a charity is a tangible way to make the world a better place – and as you can see in this chapter, it isn't something you have to be a millionaire to do. You can also make a huge difference by being a bit more environmentally conscious, so that future generations can be lucky enough to witness how beautiful the world can be. The great thing is that you can also convince your friends to get on board, by posting about the causes you care about on social media.

LIGHTS UP

How to embrace your confidence

86

From stage to set

Harry is the definition of a multi-hyphenate, someone who has several professions or skills. We all adore his music, the way he can immaculately throw an outfit together, but Harry is a man of many talents, as he is now a certified actor too.

People had long speculated that Harry was going to make the leap into acting, but it wasn't until March 2016 that it was confirmed that the musician was going to star in acclaimed director Christopher Nolan's film *Dunkirk*. The film was about the evacuation of Allied soldiers from the Dunkirk beaches of France during the Second World War, and Harry starred as young British soldier Alex.

It was a part in a prestigious film, and regardless of his high profile, it wasn't a walk in the park for Harry to get the role. Those working on the film have said they didn't see it as a positive, recruiting a famous popstar – quite the opposite, in fact. The casting director, John Papsidera, told the *Mirror*, 'We thought he was fresh and interesting and he won the role. It wasn't because he's a well-known popstar – if anything, that was more of a detriment, because it could bring the wrong message and we don't want people pulled out of the film because of who they are.' He added that Harry won the role over far more established actors and 'fought hard' for it, and that 'his work was impressive and that's what attracted us to him'.

Before the film premiered, it's fair to say some were sceptical about Styles's part, with people thinking things like, 'He's just a boy-band member, what's he doing in a war film?' But Harry proved the doubters wrong. Film critics were also positive about Harry, noting that he managed to blend into the cast seamlessly. (Quite an achievement, given his level of fame!) *USA Today* said he had a 'surprising amount of grit and pathos', while *Rolling Stone* said he played a 'small role with subtle grace and zero popstar showboating'. Praise indeed.

With his role in *Dunkirk* behind him, Harry is now moving on to more exciting projects. He will star as Jack in thriller *Don't Worry Darling* alongside Oscar-nominee Florence Pugh, who will be playing Jack's wife, Alice. The film is being directed by *Booksmart* director Olivia Wilde, who was very complimentary about Harry after filming, saying 'he blew us away every day with his talent' and 'warmth' – and 'his ability to drive backwards'. (Harry is reportedly dating Olivia after the pair worked together.) He is also set to star in *My Policeman*, a screen adaption of the LBGTQ+ novel of the same name by Bethan Roberts, along with *The Crown* actress Emma Corrin. Put it this way, we wouldn't be surprised if we soon see Harry adding a BAFTA to his BRIT Award.

Oh, and as if acting and singing aren't enough for him, Harry is also a comedian – which he proved when he had the honour of guest-hosting American sketch show *Saturday Night Live* in 2019. In the extremely funny – and sometimes slightly inappropriate – sketches, Harry did everything from acing an Icelandic accent to pretending to be a dog. Regardless of the weirdness at times, the show went down a storm. Even Forbes asked, 'Why Harry Styles Might be the Most Loved *Saturday Night Live* Host Ever.'

Getting out of your comfort zone

Obviously, Harry would never have got the part in *Dunkirk* if he didn't take a risk and try something entirely new. 'I really loved being the new guy, to be honest,' he said, speaking about his time on the *Dunkirk* set. 'I loved kinda being so far out from my comfort zone. It felt really good to kinda have no idea what I was doing for a little bit.'

We know stepping outside your comfort zone can be petrifying, but doing things that make you nervous can have incredible long-term benefits. The more you do something new – in Harry's case, acting – the less nerve-racking it becomes. The first time you do a presentation at school or work is always going to feel a lot more frightening than the fifth or sixth time. Who knows? You might even start to enjoy it when you're feeling less scared! Saying yes to things that slightly frighten you will also undoubtedly improve your self-confidence – and who doesn't want that?

The best thing is, there are small ways you can move out of your comfort zone every day – it doesn't have to be an instant, drastic change:

1. Say yes to something you wouldn't usually do: whether that's trying a new food or hanging out with a new group of friends.
2. Watch something new you wouldn't usually click on, listen to some music you wouldn't usually find on your playlists (maybe look to some of Harry's favourite acts)

or try reading a book you'd previously judged not of interest by its cover.

3. If you feel like you spend a bit too much time on your phone, you could switch it off for a while and put it in another room when you're at home to have a little digital detox. (Obviously, don't do this if you're not at home – you'll worry people if they can't get hold of you!)

4. Try to learn a new skill you think you might not be very good at – and don't put pressure on yourself to excel at it, just enjoy the process. This could be juggling – something Harry's good at! – knitting or learning a new language (another thing Harry has tried).

Lights up

Even before Harry's foray into acting, he struggled with confidence issues. It's pretty hard to believe that one of the members of the most idolised boy band of the twenty-first century didn't always feel like he was good enough, but it's true. Which is probably something to remember when you feel a little bit under the weather – everyone has their down days, or things they don't feel confident about. In the One Direction autobiography *Who We Are*, Harry writes that he wasn't always comfortable with appearing onstage. 'I'm naturally a fairly confident person in most situations, but not all,' Harry writes. 'At that point any natural confidence I had was being taken over by nerves because back then I had no idea how to channel and control my anxiety.' He added that, over time, he was able to control his nerves and learn when, and why, they hit.

Getting butterflies in your stomach will always be a weird feeling, but why do we get nervous? Well, nerves are a normal part of our body's response system to something we think is going to threaten us – this could be a speech, a job interview or a first date, for example – and our body then increases its adrenaline production. Which is why your heart starts beating faster and your breathing gets quicker. Your body is in fight-or-flight mode.

Getting nervous before some situations is totally normal, but for those who deal with anxiety, you might feel extremely nervous without an obvious cause. If you think this applies to you, visit your GP – as there are ways to make anxiety more manageable for you. And, of course, there's no shame in asking for help.

There are things you can do to try to boost your confidence before a big event, though:

- If you're feeling really nervous, talk about it to someone you trust – you'll already feel a little bit better for getting it off your chest.
- Think positive – don't think about how everything could go wrong. Visualise how it could go right.
- Remember that everyone – even Harry! – gets nervous sometimes. And it's always helpful to remember that nobody else cares as much as you think when you slip up (literally and metaphorically).

BELIEVE
IN
YOURSELF.
YOU ARE
WONDERFUL
AND
CAPABLE

Remember that making mistakes is a crucial part of growth for everyone. Even people with the biggest success stories will have got it wrong at times. The difference is that they have persevered. Remember that Liam Payne failed to make it to the live shows on *The X Factor* when he was 14 – if he hadn't tried again, he wouldn't have been in One Direction!

Stand in a power pose before you do something scary (kind of like how Harry confidently poses on the cover of his second album, *Fine Line*). According to experts, good posture can create hormones in the brain that make you feel more self-assured.

Little things

Sometimes, even when you're not stepping out onstage, you could do with a confidence boost. Low self-esteem – having a low opinion of yourself – can hit everyone from time to time. This is especially true in the age of social media, when it looks like everyone is living their best life on Instagram 24/7. It can be difficult to remember that nobody is smiling all the time – but here are some other things that might help to improve your self-esteem.

- Only follow accounts on social media that bring you joy. If somebody makes you feel bad every time you open up your Instagram app, you can unfollow them. If you're worried you might offend someone you know by unfollowing them, you can always mute them instead.

- In real life, try to spend time with people who are positive and enthusiastic – not those who bring you down or try to embarrass you.
- Do something creative – it could be anything you enjoy – that will remind you just how talented you are. We all have different strengths, and everybody is good at something.
- Mindfulness can also be used to help improve self-esteem, with some experts thinking it can improve acceptance, compassion and positive emotions. If you don't know where to start with mindfulness, there are lots of apps available.
- Exercise or yoga can help release endorphins to improve your mood. Don't worry, it doesn't have to be anything too strenuous. A walk with your friends is still getting the blood flowing around your body.
- Write down the things you like about yourself below to challenge any negative thoughts … It could be that you're a really thoughtful friend, that you have a lovely smile, that you are quick-witted. Also write down when other people say nice things about you – sometimes it's easier for other people to hype you up, and when you feel down you can look back at all the lovely things other people think about you.

_____

_____

_____

_____

_____

_____

Even the most confident people, like Harry, can become sick with nerves. But the more you do things that are out of your comfort zone, like speaking onstage or learning new skills, the easier it will be – you'll probably end up saying yes to even more challenges, and who knows where that will take you? You could even end up in a hit film ... So, like Harry, take a risk – that's usually when the best things happen. But remember that, in order to take these risks, you have to believe in yourself. You are wonderful and capable!

CHERRY

Harry's positive
approach to
relationships
and celebrity
friendships

There's absolutely no doubt that Harry Styles is a very popular man. If having literally millions of fans isn't enough proof of just how loved he is, he also has a lot of friends who think the world of him. And he has many mates that he loves just as much. In his 2019 *Guardian* interview it says that, following the One Direction hiatus, Harry set himself three goals: 'prioritise friends, learn how to be an adult, achieve a proper balance between the big and the small'.

Speaking in his *Vogue* interview, he also credited his friends with helping him get through lockdown. Living with a pod of friends in LA, which included some of his new bandmates, Harry says they would put their names in a hat to help plan their days – '[if] you were Monday, you would choose the movie, dinner and the activity for that day'. A fun idea if you want to mix your week up, maybe! 'I honestly just like being around my friends,' Harry added. 'That's been my biggest takeaway. Just being on my own the whole time, I would have been miserable.'

How to be a better friend

As Harry knows, friendships are truly one of the most magical things in life – the famous saying is that friends are the family you choose. Your relationships with your mates should be cherished and nurtured, in the same way they should honour, respect and love you. Like Harry, you should prioritise them. We're sure you're a great mate, but there are always ways you can be a better friend. Most people learn how to become a better friend throughout their whole life!

'I honestly just like being around my friends. That's been my biggest takeaway. Just being on my own the whole time, I would have been miserable.'

- Always make sure you honour the big occasions in your friends' lives and make a big deal of them. Whether that's getting a new job or acing an exam, that's cause for you to be happy for them! Remember, even if you're a tiny bit envious (a normal human emotion), you're on their team – and if you don't recognise when they've done well, your friend might feel hurt. Just because other people can have successes, doesn't mean you can't too! Success isn't finite.
- Give thoughtful presents. They don't have to cost a lot of money; maybe you could give your favourite photo together in a frame, or a collage of their favourite things, or bake something for them. Sometimes cards with a lovely message inside, can mean as much if not more than an expensive gift.
- Apologise when you have done wrong and mean it. (This is another time when a thoughtful gift wouldn't go amiss.)
- Listen to your friends and ask them thoughtful questions. If you know they're going through a tough time, regular reminders that you're there for them could make all the difference.

But if you feel like a friend doesn't respect you or value your relationship, then maybe it's time to have an honest, kind conversation with them about how you're feeling. If nothing changes after this, maybe it's time to evaluate whether you still want to be friends with them. Sometimes, friendships don't last forever – and that's OK if it means you're not getting the love and respect you deserve.

Harry's showbiz circle

Two of Harry's most famous friends are Adele and James Corden. In fact, they're such good mates, they went on holiday together in Anguilla. And while they were dining at Caribbean Fish Market just after the New Year in 2020, Harry tipped $2,020 to the bartender who served them. (See, another random act of kindness!)

Of course, one of the friendships of Harry's we love the most is his bond with pop superstar Lizzo. The pair are the epitome of BFF goals (and a lot of people wished they'd become a couple). They covered each other's songs in the BBC Radio 1 Live Lounge – Harry: 'Juice'; Lizzo: 'Adore You' – and then they took each other to the BRIT Awards. With Lizzo wearing a resplendent blue sequin dress and Harry rocking a yellow suit with a purple organza blouse, they both looked like the most fashionable pair in the room. Harry's also great mates with rapper Stormzy, who has joined him onstage, and country singer Kacey Musgraves, who joined Harry on tour.

Radio 1 presenter Nick Grimshaw is another of Harry's close mates, and one of the reasons Harry's programme *Harry Styles at the BBC* was so great was because of his friendship with Nick – the pair went to play bingo with some pensioners (which was hilarious, as some of the elderly residents of the care home just weren't too fussed about global superstar Harry – can you imagine?).

Oh, and he's also friends with Fleetwood Mac music legend Stevie Nicks. Casual! Harry even inducted Stevie – who has called him 'the son she never had' – into the Rock

& Roll Hall of Fame. It's even cooler when you consider that Harry is a fan of Fleetwood Mac. In fact, the pair only met because Harry and his sister, Gemma, went to see the band play in London back in 2015 – Harry met Stevie backstage, and because he knew it was her birthday he bought her a cake. (In case you needed any more proof that Harry is thoughtful.)

Speaking to *Vogue*, Stevie has also revealed one of the reasons why Harry is so loved by his friends – he makes them laugh, and he doesn't act like a famous diva behind closed doors. 'He's so talented, he is a really, really great artist, and he's so funny,' the 72-year-old said. 'When you're with Harry Styles, you're not with a famous person, he's just Harry.'

Admittedly, we can't all bump into famous friends – even though we would totally love to go to showbiz parties with Harry and Lizzo! But there are a few tips you can bring into your life if you would like to make more friends. And let's be honest, who doesn't want a few new mates?

1. Be yourself. Don't ever change your personality to try to make mates. You're fabulous as you are. If people can't recognise how great you are, then that's their problem.
2. Go to events you're interested in, whether that's an extra-curricular activity or a sports or music club. You will already have something in common with the people there.

Harry's love life

Harry has always been extremely private about his love life, which, at his level of fame, is completely understandable. Anybody Harry's connected with, even if they're a normal person, would instantly become a celebrity. And that's a lot to ask of a potential partner! He summed up how private he is about his relationships in an interview with the *Guardian*. When the journalist asked why he doesn't go out with 'normal people', he simply responded: 'I do. I have a private life. You just don't know about it.' Points to Harry. Despite his privacy, there have been reports about some of the more high-profile people he's dated. At the time of writing, it's believed he's currently with film director Olivia Wilde, who worked with him on *Don't Worry Darling*. In January 2021, it seemed they confirmed their romance when they arrived at his agent's wedding holding hands.

And who could forget when Harry went out with Taylor Swift from late 2012 to 2013? One of their first dates was photographed by the paparazzi in New York's Central Park. And some good music came out of it: it's believed Taylor's

'HE IS A REALLY, REALLY, REALLY GREAT ARTIST, AND HE'S SO FUNNY'

'Style' and 'Out of the Woods' are about their relationship. When he was asked about this by *Rolling Stone*, he had a typically gracious response. 'I mean, I don't know if they're about me or not,' he said, 'but the issue is, she's so good, they're everywhere. I write from my experiences; everyone does that. I'm lucky if everything [we went through] helped create those songs.' Harry is very gracious when it comes to speaking about his exes – which is something we should all definitely learn from. It can be all too easy to trash talk someone who used to be your whole world, but Harry has never gone down that route, continuing to keep his business private, even after break-ups have happened.

He also continues to stay friends with his ex-partners, which is lovely. Harry is believed to have had an on–off relationship with supermodel and *Keeping Up with the Kardashians* star Kendall Jenner, but that hasn't stopped the pair from remaining close friends. In fact, their friendship is so strong that they reunited on *The Late Late Show*. Kendall even asked which songs on his first album were about her! Instead of answering the question, Harry instead decided to tuck into a disgusting plate of food. Gross for him, but it probably ended up being a lot less embarrassing for Kendall in the long run – as even now nobody knows for sure which (if any) songs are about her.

However, probably the ultimate sign that he respects his exes is the song 'Cherry' – as, at the end of the song, a voicemail from his ex-girlfriend Camille Rowe, speaking in French, plays. Speaking with Zane Lowe on Apple Music, Harry confirmed he had actually asked Camille for her permission (though he didn't specify it was her), as he felt like the song needed the voicemail to be complete. 'We're friends and stuff, so I asked her if it was OK,' he said. 'And she was OK with it. I think she liked it.' Camille must have really respected Harry to let him do that.

Break-ups are so difficult. Whether it's your first one or not, they're never going to be a walk in the park, no matter how long the relationship has lasted for. A lot of the time it can feel like you're losing your best friend, which can seem like double the loss. Obviously, it's your own personal decision whether you want to remain friends with someone after a break-up. It depends how they treated you, and whether they would also like to be friends with you. If you don't want to hang out with them anymore, that's totally fine. But it is possible to stay friends with an ex – even if some people don't think it's the best idea! If you need an example to back you up when explaining why you want to do this, then Harry's positive relationships with his exes is all the evidence you need! It might take time, though – and that's OK. Your ex will probably need time, too.

- There's a reason people eat ice cream and chocolate after break-ups! Sometimes, that's what you need to give you a boost. And cry if you need to, there's no shame in that.
- Reach out to a friend or family member if you need to. Everyone can relate to how bleak and horrible break-ups can be.
- Play some Harry and remember that this break-up doesn't define you or take anything away from the brilliant human you are. Harry knows break-ups hurt, and that's why he's used them as inspiration for his work.

Also remember that romantic relationships don't define anyone. It can be great to have a partner, but at the same time you don't need another person to complete you. Like family, friends are some of the most important relationships you will have in your life – and it's worth investing time and energy into all of your relationships.

LITTLE THINGS

Harry's recommendations

It's fair to say that Harry Styles is a bookworm. But, like a lot of avid readers, it was only something he grew into when he was a bit older (no shame in that, by the way). He regularly talks about the literature that inspires him, but he admitted in an interview that it wasn't always this way – and that reading wasn't really his 'thing' until an ex-girlfriend gave him some books. 'I felt like I had to read them because she'd think I was a dummy if I didn't,' he told *Rolling Stone*. (OMG, imagine Harry Styles reading a book you recommended? Anyway, let's not get ahead of ourselves …) Here are some of Harry's favourite books, which might surprise you.

LOVE IS A MIXTAPE, BY ROB SHEFFIELD

Harry Styles's superfans will recognise the name Rob Sheffield, as the writer has interviewed Harry for *Rolling Stone*. Rob is a contributing editor to the magazine and, like us, he's a big Harry fan. But that isn't why Harry loves this book so much, which is a memoir following the love story between Rob and his wife, Renée (who tragically passed away five years after their wedding); each chapter starts with a mixtape, which corresponds to the plot. Harry told Timothée Chalamet that this would be one of his picks if he had to choose a book to read for the rest of his life, with Harry describing the novel as 'really beautiful'.

MY POLICEMAN, BY BETHAN ROBERTS

Harry was spotted with this book in his pocket in a photo with a fan, around the same time rumours were swirling that Harry was going to be starring in the film adaptation. Thankfully, the whispers were true – Harry will be featuring in the film as Tom, alongside *The Crown*'s Emma Corrin as Marion. The book follows an affair in Brighton in the 1950s, when male homosexuality was illegal. Tom, the policeman, is gay – but he marries Marion, a teacher, and later starts an affair with a man named Patrick.

'NOTES ON "CAMP"', BY SUSAN SONTAG

We couldn't compile this list without including the essay that inspired the wonderful Met Gala Harry co-chaired in 2019. The essay, first published in 1964, explores the meanings of the word 'camp' and is considered to be one of the first works of criticism to break down the boundaries between 'high' and 'low' culture. Camp, of course, is one of the words that can be used to describe Harry's playful style.

IN WATERMELON SUGAR, BY RICHARD BRAUTIGAN

A-ha! Does this title seem familiar to you? Thought so! During his Tiny Desk Session concert for National Public Radio (NPR), Harry confirmed that 'Watermelon Sugar' was inspired by the novel (or rather, it was in the room when he was coming up with the track). 'We had this chorus/melody, which was pretty repetitive, and a Richard Brautigan book, *In Watermelon Sugar,* was on the table and I was like, "That'll sound cool."' The book focuses on a post-apocalyptic civilisation, where many things are made out of watermelon sugar. Surreal, to say the least.

SIDDHARTHA, BY HERMANN HESSE

'A friend gave me *Siddhartha* by Hermann Hesse when we started travelling together. It makes a lot of sense to me,' Harry said in his interview with *Another Man*. 'I think it's a really important book.' The novel covers the spiritual journey of self-discovery of a man named Siddhartha, living in India at the same time as the Buddha.

LOVE IS A DOG FROM HELL, BY CHARLES BUKOWSKI

While we wouldn't ever recommend throwing something at someone onstage, a sign of Harry's love of Bukowski was when a fan chucked a book of his poems onstage during a One Direction concert. Some of Bukowski's work is very erotic. Harry is quoted in the *Sun* as describing it as 'so real, gritty and filthy, yet there is something so romantic about it all'.

THE COURSE OF LOVE, BY ALAIN DE BOTTON

Harry loves Alain de Botton so much that he turned up to his US *Vogue* interview wearing a sweatshirt with the philosopher on it, which he had designed himself. The pair met at a party, and Alain even said in an interview with *Metro* that he wanted Harry 'to go on television and recommend to everyone they read Proust and Hegel'. Harry reflected on *The Course of Love*, a book about the course of a long-term relationship after marriage, during the *Vogue* interview: 'When it comes to relationships, you just expect yourself to be good at it ... [but] being in a real relationship with someone is a skill.'

NORWEGIAN WOOD, BY HARUKI MURAKAMI

In his interview with *Rolling Stone,* Harry described this title – which is named after The Beatles' song – as 'the first book, maybe ever, where all I wanted to do all day was read this'. The story starts when the main character, Toro, hears a cover of the title track when he's arrived in Germany, which makes him think back to the 1960s. After one of Toro's friends takes his own life, readers see him develop relationships with two very different women.

THE LIFE-CHANGING MAGIC OF TIDYING, BY MARIE KONDO

Following the 2019 Met Gala, it was reported that Harry was spotted at the Strand bookstore in New York City buying multiple copies of this bestselling book by Marie Kondo. If you haven't already read the book, you're probably familiar with the title, as the book ignited a decluttering phenomenon worldwide. If you've ever heard someone say, 'Does this spark joy?' then you have Marie to thank – she even has her own Netflix show, *Tidying Up with Marie Kondo*.

THE WHITE ALBUM, BY JOAN DIDION

Harry has described a Gucci scent that he is the face of as 'what I imagine Joan Didion's house to smell like'. So he's certainly a big fan of the author. (In fact, it was also reported that when he was at the Strand bookstore he picked up numerous copies of Joan's book, *The Year of Magical Thinking*.) *The White Album* – named after The Beatles' album – is a collection of essays that examines the key events, figures and trends of the 1960s.

There you have it. Poetry, marriage and a lot of Beatles references. You can't say the musician doesn't have a varied bookshelf.

HARRY FOR EVERY MOOD

Music to live by

Need a playlist for almost every mood imaginable? Don't worry, Harry has you covered.

WHEN YOU'RE FEELING LET DOWN BY THE NEWS ...

'SIGN OF THE TIMES': If a breaking news notification has ruined your day, or you just want a break from the news altogether, this song can help you feel a little bit less lost. Sometimes it's OK to take a break from the news for five minutes if you're feeling a bit overwhelmed.

WHEN IT'S TIME TO GET THE PARTY STARTED ...

'MIDNIGHT MEMORIES': You might not be arriving anywhere by plane or staying in a fancy hotel, but One Direction's 'Midnight Memories' is perfect for when an adventure with your friends is just about to begin. Or when you just want to dance around your bedroom. Your call.

WHEN YOU'RE FEELING A BIT REBELLIOUS ...

'KIWI': This song is incredible for when you're feeling like a bit of a rebel. We recommend watching the music video again, too. There's puppies and food fights – what's not to love? However, we don't recommend smoking or drinking excessively. We promise that's something Harry wouldn't want you to start.

WHEN YOU'RE WALLOWING
IN BEING SINGLE ...

'TO BE SO LONELY': From time to time we all need to wallow in our feelings a bit, eat some ice cream and listen to sad music – especially if we're feeling a bit lonely. But remember, being single is completely OK. You don't need anybody else to be complete or content. Plus, there are a lot of pros to being single. (The first one being that you don't have to share your ice cream with anyone.)

WHEN YOU NEED TO TACKLE
THE GREEN-EYED MONSTER ...

'WOMAN': OK, so we all know jealousy isn't a nice trait. Back in the 1600s, Shakespeare told us to beware of the green-eyed monster. But jealousy is human. Even the most self-assured people can feel a bit jealous. Including Harry, who is thought to have written this song about an ex's new partner. So listen to this and know you're not alone. Feeling a bit jealous is fine, so long as you don't take it out on anyone else. And remember that you're enough as you are.

WHEN YOU HAVE A MASSIVE CRUSH ...

'ADORE YOU': You know when you think someone is so fantastic you can't stop thinking about them? When you smile every time they text you? When your friends are bored of how much you talk about them? Then 'Adore You' is totally the song for how you're feeling. Harry himself says the uplifting track is about 'that initial infatuation stage, that heavy feeling, which is bliss, I guess'. Don't worry, we've all been there.

117

WHEN YOU'RE TRYING NOT TO
GO THROUGH YOUR EX'S INSTAGRAM ...

'CHERRY': Instagram can be the best for keeping in contact with your friends. But it can be the worst if you get the inclination to stalk an ex. Especially if they've moved on with someone else and they're posting #relationshipgoals photos. Ergh! We recommend that you try to avoid their profile, and listen to this heartbreaking ballad instead, which is believed to feature a voicemail from Harry's ex, the French model Camille Rowe.

WHEN YOU'RE IN NEED
OF A SELF-ESTEEM BOOST ...

'GOLDEN': Need some confidence to tackle that project at work or school? Not feeling 100 per cent yourself? Sounds like you need reminding of your badass self and how utterly fabulous you are. And this shimmery track is bound to do that. As Harry says, you are golden – take that as a sign and put your best foot forward.

WHEN YOU'RE FEELING NOSTALGIC ...

'WHAT MAKES YOU BEAUTIFUL': It might not be your personal favourite One Direction song – or maybe it is! – however, as their first single, it is the track that kickstarted everything. Nostalgia aside, it's also perfect if you need an empowering pick-me-up. No matter your insecurities, One Direction will always think you are beautiful – inside and out. Remember that!

WHEN YOU JUST WANT
TO BE AT THE BEACH ...

'WATERMELON SUGAR': It could be freezing cold and pouring with rain, but this song just about has the power to make you feel like you're at a gorgeous beach, soaking up the sun, eating a fruit salad. 'Watermelon Sugar' feels like going on holiday without a care in the world or having fun at a festival with your friends. It also helps that it's the catchiest song in the entire world. Thanks, Harry!

WHEN YOU WAKE UP
ON THE WRONG SIDE OF BED ...

'DRAG ME DOWN': In a grumpy, grouchy mood? You need cheering up, fast. Let us direct you to 'Drag Me Down', which will turn your mood upside down – in the best way possible, of course.

WHEN YOU NEED
TO MAKE UP WITH SOMEONE ...

'SWEET CREATURE': When you've fallen out with a friend or partner, it can feel like one of the worst things in the world. Especially if you want to make up with them, and you think you might have to swallow your pride and apologise. Listen to the lyrics to this dreamy track and you might have the confidence to reach out and make amends. Harry has previously said it's sometimes easier to communicate by song, and that 'Sweet Creature' wrapped up everything he needed to say to someone in three and a half minutes.

WHEN YOU JUST WANT TO DAYDREAM ...

'SHE': Headphones on, 'She' is perfect for when your head's in the clouds, as Harry sings about being in daydreams with someone. We totally wish it was us – but we guess listening to this will have to do.

AND A SONG FOR EVERY OTHER MOOD ...

'TREAT PEOPLE WITH KINDNESS': Not quite sure how you're feeling? If all else fails, stick 'TPWK' on loud and proud. After all, this joyous anthem is the song Harry lives his entire life by. If you're feeling ambitious, you could even try to learn the Old Hollywood-inspired dance routine from the video ... We're sure Harry would be impressed.

QUIZZES

How Harry are you?

We know you're a Harry fan – obviously, who isn't? – but just how Harry are you really? Do you know your Met Galas from your BRIT Awards, your Gucci from your Moschino, your Stevie Nicks from your David Bowie? Do you know how to style an outfit and take a fashion risk? But, most importantly, do you treat people with kindness? Take the test below to find out, and try to refrain from cheating – we're putting our trust in you!

DESCRIBE YOUR STYLE IN A NUTSHELL ...
a.   Chic, minimalist, smart
b.   A mix of staple styles, with a few eye-catching pieces
c.   Fierce, flamboyant and fearless

IF YOU HAD TO SPLURGE ON A DESIGNER ITEM, WHICH STORE WOULD YOU VISIT?
a.   Chanel
b.   Moschino
c.   Gucci

YOU'RE PICKING OUT A SHOE TO COMPLETE THE PERFECT OUTFIT. YOU GO FOR ...
a.   A pair of Louboutin heels
b.   Converse trainers
c.   Heeled boots

WHO WOULD BE YOUR CELEBRITY BFF ...?

a. Meghan Markle
b. Katy Perry
c. Lizzo

YOU'RE BINGEING SOMETHING ON NETFLIX, WHAT DO YOU PICK?

a. *Emily In Paris*
b. *Game of Thrones*
c. *Fleabag*

YOU HAVE TO PICK YOUR FAVOURITE FILM ...

a. *Breakfast at Tiffany's*
b. *The Great Gatsby*
c. *Love Actually*

IF YOU COULD GO ANYWHERE ON HOLIDAY, WHERE WOULD YOU GO?

a. Paris
b. New York
c. Tokyo

IF YOU COULD SEE ANYONE — APART FROM HARRY, OF COURSE! — IN CONCERT, WHO WOULD IT BE?

a. Ed Sheeran
b. Billie Eilish
c. Fleetwood Mac

IF YOU HAD TO PICK A MEAL AT A RESTAURANT ...

a. Steak and very finely cut chips
b. Pizza
c. Sweetcorn and tacos

YOU'VE GOT A LAZY AFTERNOON, YOU DECIDE TO ...

a. Have a long bath
b. Cook
c. Learn a new language

YOU HAVE TO SHOWCASE YOUR BEST PARTY TRICK, YOU DECIDE TO ...

a. Pirouette
b. Ride a unicycle
c. Juggle, and then launch into playing the kazoo

EEK! YOU HAVE TO ADMIT YOUR BIGGEST FEAR ...

a. The dark
b. Spoons
c. Snakes – I'd be completely useless in an *I'm a Celebrity* ... Bushtucker Trial

YOU'RE CHOOSING A TATTOO, WHAT DO YOU GO FOR?

a. What?! I'd never get a tattoo!
b. A planet
c. A mermaid

WHAT WAS THE LAST THING YOU POSTED ON INSTAGRAM?

a. A mirror selfie, wearing a gorgeous pair of shades and a coordinated outfit

b. A group Polaroid snap with all my friends

c. A picture in my finest suit, in a not-so-serious pose

IF YOUR FRIEND NEEDED CHEERING UP, YOU WOULD ...

a. Write them a thoughtful postcard

b. Give them a call and check in

c. Drop everything to go and see them – my friends are the most important thing in the world, after all

MOSTLY AS

You are so chic, my friend! You are too cool for school, which is by no means a bad thing. But you still have a little way to go before you're Harry Styles-endorsed cool. Not to panic, you'll soon be on your way after listening to some vintage One Direction.

MOSTLY BS

We want to invite you to a party, we reckon you'd be great fun – and not just for your party skill of riding a unicycle! You love anything bright and fun, just like Harry. But you're not entirely there yet ... Maybe get listening to some Fleetwood Mac, Joni Mitchell and David Bowie, and then go thrift shopping if you really want to move up a level in the Harry stakes.

MOSTLY CS

Wait a minute, are you sure you're not Harry reading
this book? You embody Harry so well that we wouldn't be
surprised if we see you on the cover of *Vogue*, or onstage
singing to thousands. With Lizzo right by your side.
So keep doing what you're doing, and continue to TPWK.

'SMALL CHANGES END UP MAKING A BIG DIFFER-ENCE'

How well do you know Harry?

So, you've read the book, but the real question is: have you been paying attention? How much do you really know about Harry? Get your pen ready for the ultimate test, featuring facts, figures and languages.

I. WHAT YEAR WAS HARRY BORN?

a. 1996

b. 1998

c. 1993

d. 1994

2. WHAT WAS THE NAME OF THE BAKERY HARRY USED TO WORK AT?

a. Stephenson Bakery

b. Mandeville Bakery

c. Sugar, Spice, All Things Nice

d. Great Bakes, Cheshire

3. WHICH JUDGE DIDN'T BELIEVE IN HARRY DURING HIS FIRST AUDITION?

a. Louis Walsh

b. Simon Cowell

c. Sinitta

d. Nicole Scherzinger

4. WHAT WAS THE NAME OF THE FIRST SONG ONE DIRECTION PERFORMED TOGETHER ON THE X FACTOR?

a.   Natalie Imbruglia – 'Torn'
b.   Coldplay – 'Viva La Vida'
c.   P!nk – 'Nobody Knows'
d.   Bryan Adams – 'Summer of '69'

5. WHICH MUSICAL ICON INSPIRED HARRY TO RELEASE 'TREAT PEOPLE WITH KINDNESS'?

a.   Prince
b.   David Bowie
c.   Freddie Mercury
d.   Tom Jones

6. WHO WAS NOT A CO-HOST FOR THE 2019 MET GALA?

a.   Rihanna
b.   Lady Gaga
c.   Serena Williams
d.   Anna Wintour

7. WHAT YEAR DID HARRY CUT HIS HAIR FOR THE LITTLE PRINCESS TRUST?

a.   2013
b.   2016
c.   2014
d.   2019

8. HOW MUCH MONEY FOR CHARITY DID HARRY RAISE ON HIS FIRST TOUR?

a. $1.2 million

b. $1 million

c. $0.8 million

d. $1.5 million

9. WHAT WAS THE NAME OF THE SOLDIER HARRY PLAYED IN DUNKIRK?

a. Ben

b. George

c. Adam

d. Alex

10. IN WHICH LANGUAGE IS THE VOICEMAIL FEATURED ON 'CHERRY'?

a. Spanish

b. French

c. Welsh

d. Italian

11. WHAT'S THE NAME OF ONE OF HARRY'S FAVOURITE BOOKS BY ROB SHEFFIELD?

a. *Love Is a Mixtape*

b. *The White Album*

c. *In Watermelon Sugar*

d. *Norwegian Wood*

12. WHICH OF HARRY'S FRIENDS WAS HIS DATE TO THE 2020 BRIT AWARDS?

a. Stormzy

b. Adele

c.   Stevie Nicks

d.   Lizzo

13. WHO WILL HARRY STAR ALONGSIDE IN MY POLICEMAN?

a.   Lily James

b.   Emma Corrin

c.   Lydia West

d.   Zendaya

14. WHICH CHAT-SHOW HOST DID HARRY TAKE OVER FOR WHEN HIS WIFE GAVE BIRTH?

a.   Trevor Noah

b.   Graham Norton

c.   James Corden

d.   Jimmy Kimmel

15. WHAT WAS HARRY'S FIRST TATTOO?

a.   Outline of a star

b.   Butterfly

c.   Mermaid

d.   Birdcage

ANSWERS

1 – d, 2 – b, 3 – a, 4 – a, 5 – b, 6 – a, 7 – b, 8 – a, 9 – d, 10 – b, 11 – a, 12 – d, 13 – b, 14 – c, 15 – a

How well do you know One Direction?

So, we know how well you know Harry by now – but how well do you know One Direction? Were you a Directioner? Can you recite their video diaries by heart, sing their albums backwards? Give this test a try and see how well you know each member – obviously at the same time as listening to some old-school One Direction!

1. Which One Direction star was attacked by a goat when he was 10?

2. Which member appeared on *Waterloo Road* before his time in the band?

3. Which member of One Direction has a phobia of spoons?

4. When *Up All Night* hit the charts, which member bought a mattress to celebrate the huge achievement?

5. Which member of One Direction is scared of pigeons, and faced his fear on TV?

6. Which member of One Direction was suspended from school and had to retake Year 12?

7. Which member of One Direction always used to brush their teeth before going onstage?

8. Which member of One Direction applied to be on *The X Factor* in 2009, but pulled out due to nerves?

9. Which member of One Direction was really good at sprinting, and used to regularly run five miles a day before school?

10. Which member of One Direction has a birthday on Christmas Eve?

11. Who is the youngest member of One Direction?

12. Which One Direction member's first concert was Nickelback in Manchester?

13. Which One Direction star had to miss his own prom?

14. Which One Direction star's favourite film trilogy is *Toy Story*?

15. Which One Direction member started Modest! Golf Management?

ANSWERS

1– Harry **2** – Louis **3** – Liam **4** – Harry **5** – Niall
6 – Louis **7** – Zayn **8** – Zayn **9** – Liam **10** – Louis
11 – Harry **12** – Harry **13** – Niall **14** – Liam **15** – Niall

Conclusion

We really don't want to say goodbye, but sadly this is the end of the book ... We hope you've enjoyed it and learnt some kind, helpful lessons along the way to help make your life, and other people's, brighter. Following Harry's example, we hope you do more random acts of kindness, embrace your true style and start to take more healthy risks in life. We also hope you take the time to treat everyone with kindness, by educating yourself, listening to other people's stories and being an ally. We also hope you will be inspired to help out charitable causes – whether that's through donating money or your time.

Everyone can be like Harry if they live their lives by his mantra: always treat people with kindness. But we also hope you take the time to show yourself some love, because sometimes that's the kindest thing you can do for yourself. Believe in yourself, and you will shine.

RESOURCES

ADORE YOU: A LOVE LETTER TO HARRY

Sheffield, Rob, 'Review: Harry Styles Is a True Rock Star on Superb Solo Debut', *Rolling Stone*, 12 May 2017

Finn, Natalie, 'Ariana Grande "Loves" the Song Harry Styles Wrote for Her, Talks "Insanity" of Opening the 2014 MTV VMAs', *E!*, 20 August 2014

'Timothée Chalamet in conversation with Harry Styles: the hottest actor on the planet interviewed by music's most charismatic popstar', *i-D*, 27 December 2019

Lamont, Tom, 'Harry Styles: "I'm not just sprinkling in sexual ambiguity to be interesting"', *Guardian*, 14 December 2019

Rainbird, Ashleigh, 'Can this boy get any cuter? Harry Styles buys £3,000 of pizzas and hands them out to the homeless', *Mirror*, 1 February 2013

Crowe, Cameron, 'Harry Styles' New Direction', *Rolling Stone*, 18 April 2017

Bowles, Hamish, 'Playtime with Harry Styles', *Vogue*, 13 November 2020

Sheffield, Rob, 'The Eternal Sunshine of Harry Styles', *Rolling Stone*, 26 August 2019

McDermott, Kerry, 'Rock Goddess Stevie Nicks on Insomnia, Inventing Her Own Style, and Her White Knight Harry Styles', *Vogue*, 14 October 2020

'Harry Styles steps in for James Corden to host *The Late Late Show*', *BBC Newsbeat*, 13 December 2017

HISTORY: HARRY'S JOURNEY FROM THE BAKERY TO SUPER STARDOM

Finn, Natalie, '26 Essential Things You Should Know About Harry Styles', *E! News*, 1 February 2020

Simms, Kate, 'Harry Styles has got the *X Factor* in Holmes Chapel', BBC News, 17 November 2010

Harry Styles's *X Factor* Audition (Full Version), YouTube, 19 September 2010

One Direction – The X Factor Judges' Houses – 'Torn' (Full) HD, YouTube, 9 August 2011

Bowman, Lisa, 'Harry Styles reveals he came up with the name for One Direction,' *NME*, 17 October 2017

Thompson, Sophie, 'Every One Direction *X Factor* performance ranked', *PopBuzz*, 23 July 2020

One Direction Video Diaries (ALL), YouTube, 2 April 2013

'One Direction: Ten years of 1D, but is a reunion on the way?', *Newsround*, 21 July 2020

One Direction, Wikipedia (no date)

Trust, Gary, 'One Direction Beats Beatles' Record with Fifth Top 10 Debut on Hot 100', *Billboard*, 27 October 2015

Greenwood, Douglas, 'How One Direction became the world's first internet boy band', *Independent*, 23 July 2020

Carpenter, Julie, 'The parents One Direction left behind', *Express*, 22 August 2013

Finn, Natalie, 'Remembering the Drama of the Day Zayn Malik Quit One Direction', *E! News*, 25 March 2020

Dam, Christina, 'From throwing insults to talking about a reunion, here's everything One Direction members have said since their hiatus', *Insider*, 31 December 2020

Crumlish, Callum, 'One Direction: Harry Styles doubted his own success without 1D', *Express*, 29 November 2020

McCartney, Paul, 'HARRY STYLES', *Another Man*, 7 June 2017

Halperin, Shirley, 'This Charming Man: Why We're Wild About Harry Styles', *Variety*, 2 December 2020

TREAT PEOPLE WITH KINDNESS

McLaren, Bonnie, 'When Harry Met Phoebe: The Story Behind the "Treat People with Kindness" Music Video', *Grazia*, 1 February 2021

Homewood, Ben, '"Small changes make a big difference": Harry

Styles tells the story of "Treat People with Kindness"', *Music Week*, 12 December 2019

Treat People with Kindness, Harry Styles website (no date)

Edmonds, Lizzie, 'Harry Styles "writes note for superfan and feeds her fish while she's out"', *Evening Standard*, 29 October 2020

Rao, Dr Amra, 'How being kind benefits us psychologically', The British Psychological Society, 12 June 2020

Park, Andrea, 'Harry Styles Paused His London Concert to Help a Fan Who Was Having a Panic Attack', *Teen Vogue*, 31 October 2017

Michallon, Clemence, 'Harry Styles sends fan touching message on World Mental Health Day as he hints at new album', *Independent*, 10 October 2019

'Harry Styles reveals his top tips for staying entertained during self-isolation', *MTV*, 20 March 2020

SIGN OF THE TIMES: HARRY'S STYLE SCHOOL

Pike, Naomi, 'Harry Styles Hasn't Always Worn Candy-Floss-Pink Suits and a String of Pearls', *Vogue*, 12 March 2021

'Camp: Notes on Fashion', Wikipedia

Sasso, Samantha, 'We Finally Know Who Pierced Harry Styles' Ear', *Refinery29*, 9 May 2019

Delgado, Sara, 'Harry Styles Keeps His Clothes in a Frozen Vault with 24-hour Security', *Teen Vogue*, 23 October 2019

Pike, Naomi, 'The Inside Scoop on All of Harry Styles's "Unexpected" Met Gala Looks', *Vogue*, 7 May 2019

Whitehead, Joanna, 'Harry Styles Becomes First Man to Appear Solo on Cover of Vogue', *Independent*, 13 November 2020

Roach, April, 'Harry Styles hits back at Candace Owens after she slammed his *Vogue* cover and said "bring back manly men"', *Evening Standard*, 2 December 2020

Lucas, Georgina, 'Can clothes really make you happy?' *Stylist*, 23 September 2020

'Harry Styles Donates His Clothes to Charity', *Female First*, 27 September 2015

Bhatia, Billie, 'You can now make Harry Styles' viral JW Anderson cardigan at home', *Stylist*, 3 July 2020

GOLDEN: HARRY'S LESSONS IN EQUALITY AND INCLUSION

Mamo, Heran, 'Harry Styles Endorses Joe Biden: "If I Could Vote in America, I'd Vote with Kindness"', *Billboard*, 27 October 2020

Rosenbaum, Claudia; Blackman, Michael, 'Taylor Swift's Instagram Post Has Caused a Massive Spike in Voter Registration', *BuzzFeed News*, 8 October 2018

Bailey, Alyssa, 'Harry Styles Joined a Los Angeles Black Lives Matter Protest', *ELLE*, 3 June 2020

Karlan, Sarah, 'Harry Styles Stopped Mid-Concert to Help a Fan Come Out to Her Mom', *BuzzFeed News*, 17 July 2018

'Harry Styles Drops "Bisexual Anthem" "Lights Up" on National Coming Out Day',

Capital FM, 11 October 2019

Singh, Olivia, '9 times Harry Styles was a champion for the LGBTQ community', *Insider*, 4 June 2020

Phillips, Hedy, '7 Times Harry Styles Proved He's Actually Our Feminist Prince', HelloGiggles, 1 February 2021

Rubin, Elana, 'Why Harry Styles is the artist of the decade', *Insider*, 11 December 2019

SWEET CREATURE: HOW TO MAKE A CHANGE

McFarland, Kelly, 'Wing Walking Wonder Woman Anne Twist has raised over 10K for Parkinson's UK', CelebMix, 9 October 2020

'HAPPY BIRTHDAY ANNE TWIST: A LOOK AT ALL THE TIMES SHE'S SUPPORTED CHARITY', TBHonest, 21 October 2020

Maine, Samantha, 'Harry Styles raised $1.2 million for charity during his world tour', *NME*, 20 July 2018

'Harry Styles cuts his famous hair for charity', *HELLO!*, 7 May 2016

'Volunteering and its Surprising Benefits', HelpGuide

LIGHTS UP: HOW TO EMBRACE YOUR CONFID ENCE

Feinstein, Sharon, 'Harry Styles tipped for Hollywood success over his performance in war epic *Dunkirk*', *Mirror*, 28 May 2016

Mandell, Andrea, 'Everything critics are saying about Harry Styles in *Dunkirk*', *USA Today*, 20 July 2017

Lavin, Will, 'Olivia Wilde shares first-look image of Harry Styles in new film *Don't Worry Darling*', *NME*, 16 February 2021

Spranklen, Annabelle, 'Emma Corrin and Harry Styles are starring in this new Amazon film about a "heartbreaking love triangle"', *Glamour*, 5 February 2020

Chang, Rachel, 'Why Harry Styles Might be the Most Loved Saturday Night Live Host Ever', *Forbes*, 25 November 2019

Hegarty, Tasha, 'Harry Styles loved being "out of his comfort zone" on the set on *Dunkirk*', *Digital Spy*, 9 April 2017

Nagi, Ariel, 'Even Harry Styles Has Struggled with Self-Confidence: "I Had No Idea How to Control My Anxiety"' *Seventeen*, 23 September 2014

'Nervousness: How You Can Deal with It and Feel Better', Healthline (no date)

'Raising low self-esteem', NHS (no date)

CHERRY: HARRY'S POSITIVE APPROACH TO RELATION SHIPS AND CELEBRITY FRIEND SHIPS

'Harry Styles Celebrity Friends: Inside His Inner Showbiz Circle', Capital FM, 31 December 2020

'Inside Harry Styles & Fleetwood Mac Star Stevie Nicks's Incredible Friendship', Capital FM, 25 November 2020

Willen, Claudia, 'Harry Styles shared a voicemail from his ex on a new song and a fan translated it from French to English', *Insider*, 13 December 2019

Bailey, Alyssa, 'Harry Styles Is Now Happy to Discuss Taylor Swift's Songs About Him', *ELLE*, 2 March 2020

LITTLE THINGS: HARRY'S RECOMMEN-DATIONS

Edwards, Jack, 'Read every
     book Harry Styles has
     recommended and his taste is
     immaculate *My Policeman*
     I SEE YOU' YouTube,
     28 December 2020

Roberson, Blythe, 'I Read All of
     Harry Styles' Favorite Books
     & Here's What I Learned
     About Him', *Bustle*, 30 March
     2020

Keller, Hadley, 'Is Harry Styles
     a Marie Kondo Fan?' *House
     Beautiful*, 14 May 2019

Farrell, Ally, 'Harry Styles
     reveals he loves erotic
     poetry', *Sun*, 30 September
     2016

Ramzi, Lilah, 'Harry Styles
     Really Likes Alain de Botton
     – And He Has the Sweatshirt
     [to] Prove It', *Vogue*,
     13 November 2020